STAY

threads, conversations, collaborations

Nick Flynn

PUBLISHED BY
ZE Books of Houston, TX
in partnership with Unnamed
Press of Los Angeles, CA

3262 Westheimer Road, #467
Houston, TX 77098
www.zebooks.com

CREDITS
"Amanuensis," "Unknown," "Confessional,"
and "The Unclaimed" from *I Will Destroy
You*. Copyright © 2019 by Nick Flynn. "Bag
of Mice," "Sudden," "Father Outside," "Her
Smoke (her trick)," and "Emptying Town" from
Some Ether. Copyright © 2000 by Nick Flynn.
"My Joke," "Philip Seymour Hoffman," "Put
the Load on Me," "AK-47," and "The Day Lou
Reed Died" from *My Feelings*. Copyright ©
2015 by Nick Flynn. "water," "saudade," "seven
testimonies," and "harbor" from *The Captain
Asks for a Show of Hands*. Copyright © 2011 by
Nick Flynn. "Hive" and "Swarm" from *Blind
Huber*. Copyright © 2002 by Nick Flynn. All
used with the permission of The Permissions
Company, LLC, on behalf of Graywolf Press,
graywolfpress.org.

Material in this volume adapted from *Another
Bullshit Night in Suck City*. Copyright © 2004 by
Nick Flynn. *The Ticking Is the Bomb*. Copyright ©
2010 by Nick Flynn. *The Reenactments*. Copyright
© 2013 by Nick Flynn. All used by permission of
W. W. Norton & Company, Inc.

PUBLISHER'S NOTE
Each book in this series brings
together in one place the work of
a writer or artist who has some
relationship to visual culture.

BOOK SERIES DESIGN
With Projects, Inc.
www.withprojects.org

ISBN
978-1-7335401-1-7

2 4 6 8 9 7 5 3 1
First ZE Books Printing,
March 2020

Library of Congress Control No.
2019948593

Typeset in Janson and Univers.

Printed on 55LB. Rolland Enviro
100 Natural.

Printed in Canada.

ENVIRONMENTAL BENEFITS STATEMENT
New Society Publishing saved the following resources by printing the pages of
this book on chlorine-free paper made with 100% post-consumer waste.

TREES	WATER	ENERGY	SOLID WASTE	GREENHOUSE GASES
16 Fully Grown	7,427 Gallons	8 Million BTUs	497 Pounds	1,369 Pounds

Environmental impact estimates were made using the Environmental Paper Network
Paper Calculator 3.2. For more information visit www.papercalculator.org.

for my collaborators—*impossible without*

Alice Invents a Little Game & Alice Always Wins
This Is the Night Our House Will Catch Fire
The Captain Asks for a Show of Hands
Another Bullshit Night in Suck City
A Note Slipped Under the Door
The Ticking Is the Bomb
I Will Destroy You
The Reenactments
My Feelings
Blind Huber
Some Ether
Stay

Threads

. . . like meteor showers all the time, bombardment, constant connections.

Begin

MANIFEST (O)

Each artist, each human, contains within them a closed image system, a handful of scenes they return to, again and again. Jung called them symbols and believed that as long as they were alive they kept spinning off meaning.

In hindsight I can see that in each of my books there are certain images that keep showing up, repeating. Let's call them *threads of thought*.

> *A man putting himself into a trashbag.*
> *A mother contemplating her gun.*
> *A child in pajamas on the lawn outside a*
> *house on fire.*

These are some of the images, mostly from my childhood, still lodged inside me. Perhaps the reason they keep appearing when I sit down to write is that I have not found a way to contain them, a way to get them out of my body. Part of our work as artists is to get as close to the source of these archetypes as possible. To deny them seems fruitless.

> *Donuts. Orange plastic pill*
> *bottles. A saltwater marsh.*

This book is an attempt to bring together these threads—those that have stayed with me, that have led me to write the books I've written, and to collaborate with the artists that have found me. This book also includes some of my collages, some of which were made when I was wandering, some made more recently, many as collaborations with my daughter, age five, six, seven . . . Within, you will also find fragments of sources, influences, conversations, and other travels in the collective unconscious.

a version of a conversation with patricia weaver
francisco & christopher vondracek, hamline
university, 2016

nick flynn, *dark thought*, 2014

Figure 6

nick flynn, *weld*, 2006

ON EPHEMERA

When I find myself in a new city or
town, at least until I know where I am,
I give myself a daily task. Each day I
must locate three (sometimes more)
pieces of ephemera—a scrap of paper,
a gum wrapper, a shopping list, a
child's drawing—with the intention of
making a collage. Ideally I will finish
the collage by the end of the day, and
the next day I will begin a new one.
To call what I'm looking for trash is
accurate, as it is usually something that
has been discarded, hopefully even
walked on, definitely exposed to the
weather, but not for too long. I like
the effects of weather on paper, how
it seems to contain time. I don't pick
through trash bins—I have to find it
underfoot. I'll spend the whole day
searching for these three scraps, with
a simultaneous task of finding a piece
of cardboard to arrange them on.
I also have to locate a stationery store,
where I can buy rubber cement,
or a glue stick. It's preferable if the
cardboard has an image printed on
it—a label indicating what the box
once held (oranges or safety pins), a
number or a logo. The scavenger hunt
helps me get through the first day
or week. I get to know the city this
way. I get to find out where or who
or what I am.

first published in *nowhere*, 2008

nick flynn, *scream*, 2015

Sleeping Beauty
(The Mother)

josh neufeld, *bag of mice*, 2007

BAG OF MICE

I dreamt your suicide note
was scrawled in pencil on a brown paperbag
& in the bag were six baby mice. The bag
opened into darkness,
smoldering
from the top down. The mice,
huddled at the bottom, scurried the bag
across a shorn field. I stood over it
& as the burning reached each carbon letter
of what you'd written
your voice released into the night
like a song, & the mice
grew wilder.

from *some ether*

ON GHOSTS

Q: Can you talk a bit about your mother, place her in the frame of your story? Do you recognize her in yourself?

A: My mother is a ghost presence in *Another Bullshit Night in Suck City*, simply because that book focuses on how the trajectory of my life and the trajectory of my father's life led us both into a homeless shelter for a few overlapping years. Yet my mother is the question behind everything we both do, hovering, both in her presence and in her absence, over us. Maybe there was no other place my father and I could have wrestled with the ghost of her but in that shelter, on those streets. And the question of how much of my mother I see in myself, I imagine we all hope that only the positive genes are passed on, but I don't think it works that way.

susan landry talks with nick flynn,
run to the roundhouse, nellie, 2014

thomas fling draper (my mother's father),
mexico, c. 1947

WATERMELONS

I have an enduring image from my childhood, one that returns to me often, unbidden. It involves a plant that somehow took root in the backseat of my grandmother's car. Collected on the floor between the seats and the doors was a mixture of sand and dirt, carried in on our feet from the beach, and as mud on our sneakers on rainy days. No one ever cleaned the dirt, not from the backseat—my grandmother never gave it much thought. When I was young I sat in the back with the groceries, watching the trees pass, pushing her dog away with my feet. The dog smelled—if you touched it, your hands smelled like dog. Over the years the soil that gathered in the space between the seats and the doors grew deep, deep enough for a seed of an unspecified plant to take hold and send up a shoot. I'd chart its growth in private, checking on it whenever we went for a ride. I don't think that I ever told her, for fear she'd uproot it. My secret.

Near the end I drove more than she did. I drove her into town for groceries or to the bank. I drove her to the dump and to the vet. If it was spring the plants would send up their green leaves, for by then there were more than one, and by the leaves they were identifiably watermelons. By then I felt safe to talk about them with her, and we'd laugh together at the weirdness of it all.

Without this image, how else can I hold her now? Her voice? (*like sandpaper & smoke*) Her hands? (*gnarled from tending her roses*) Her roses? (*in the summer they nearly swallowed her porch*).

from *a note slipped under the door*

WOOL

A loss of belief is what separates us from the much-
handled things we grew up with . . .
—D.J. Waldie, *Holy Land*

My mother's name is Jody. Her maiden name was Draper.
Draper is a name like Smith, it is the name of the thing
the people do. Smiths shoe horses. Drapers sell cloth.
Her father, my grandfather, was a wool merchant, as was
his father, and so on, all the way back.

What this meant was that we had one bag of wool
kicking around our house for as long as I could remember.
A paperbag, ten skeins of wool inside. Two blood red
needles poke out from the open top.

This is one of the much-handled things I grew up
with—a paperbag, filled with enough charcoal-gray wool
for a sweater, if my mother ever gets around to knitting
it. My grandfather had given her the wool when she'd said
she wanted to learn.

To knit. A sweater. For me.

When my grandfather was a teenager he lived, for a summer,
on a sheep farm in Montana. After the war (WWII) he
would go back to that sheep farm, now as a journeyman
merchant, to learn the family business: how to grade
the wool, how much to offer for it, who to sell it to in the
factories back east.

His youngest, his daughter (my mother), had been
born just before the war. My grandfather held her, he must
have held her, at least once, for at least a moment, before
he shipped out.

After the war he came back with this inside him:
Knee-deep in the sea, waist-deep, our guns raised
above our heads, wading toward the fire. The water slowed me,
it slowed us all. Back home my wife watched over our three
children, the youngest, a girl, I hardly knew her, I never was
able to know her, something always hung between us. Her hand
so tiny in mine, her mouth so empty, as if all her teeth had
been knocked out by the stock of a gun.

After the war, as he made his way back and forth
to Montana, she grew up—she was what they called
"rebellious" in the 1950s. My grandfather and his wife were
both drinkers, which limited their parenting skills and

options, so at some point it made sense to simply ship Jody off to boarding school.

Troubled girl, kicked out of one school after another. I think of her at times like Penelope, weaving her tapestry by day, unweaving it by night, attempting to slow time, to delay the moment she will have to decide.

Then she meets my father, gets pregnant, takes his name.

She's seventeen.

When I was a boy I'd take the P&B bus into Boston to visit my grandfather in his office. It took about an hour, it cost about two dollars. I imagine my mother bought me the ticket, but that might not be true—I did a lot on my own. The bus was silver and blue, the P stood for Plymouth (where the pilgrims landed), the B for Brockton, which was and is just another broken town to glimpse from the window of a moving bus.

The address of my grandfather's office was Ten High Street. The Draper Top Company. Top is a grade of wool suitable to knit. It has been combed, cleaned, spun into yarn. Sample skeins were lined up on a desk in his conference room, each skein had been touched by his hands, brought here from a ranch somewhere out west— by the end the wool was being imported from as far away as Australia. Some of the wool was sheep white, some dyed gray, some the black of a black sheep. Each was coiled like a tiny spool of rope, each wrapped in brown paper, a white label affixed to the paper. On the label: the date, the grade of wool, the farm of origin, all typed neatly out by his secretary.

Wool poked out from each end of the neatly wrapped skeins. Handle a skein and your hands get a little oily. The oil is what keeps the sheep dry, huddled in their field, rain and darkness falling. The oil is lanolin, it oozes from inside them, we use it to keep our hands soft, it waterproofs our boots. Each strand of wool has a tiny hook on each end, which hooks on to another strand when you roll them together. My grandfather explained this to me, using a finger from each hand to make two hooks— *Like this*, he said.

Wool merchant—even as a child I thought he was out of time, as if he sold buggy whips, or wore a top hat. His father had made a fortune during the wars, back when

all the uniforms were made of wool, all the blankets, all
the felt lining all the boots. If you had anything to do
with wool you could become rich, and my great-grandfather
did. By the time the Vietnam War was winding down,
polyester had slowly crept in, and slowly taken over.
My stepfather came home from Vietnam with a nylon
camouflaged blanket, which I would use for the rest of the
1970s—it rolled up small. Wool would get eaten by moths,
wool would end up with holes eaten into it.

When I'd visit my grandfather, in his office, or
anywhere, the first thing he'd do was touch whatever shirt
I was wearing, whatever sweater. It was the 1970s, I wore
polyester sometimes, we all did, big-collared shirts with
cityscapes printed on them, but not around him. The first
thing he'd do when I entered his office was take a sleeve
between his thumb and forefinger and rub it—in this way
he would know if the sweater was pure, or a blend.

In war no one speaks of the ones who are already down,
already on their knees, the ones not yet to the beach
and already fallen into and maybe under the water, under
the waves, which will not save them. No one speaks
of the man using his gun as a crutch, the man using his
gun as a shield, the man who has already abandoned
his weapon. None of these men will make it. Empty-
handed almost, their eyes, we will never see their eyes,
not as they move into the fire, into the smoke. Explosions
and fire and smoke, flashes of light which signal a death,
then another. The water is up to our waists, which is good,
as we are pissing ourselves empty. I hold the gun above
my head, we all have the same rifle. We all have the same
helmet, we all have the same boots, we are a unit and
we move as a unit through the waist-deep sea. Waist-deep
a hundred yards from shore, we hold our rifles above
the water, we move as one, in our wool suits, the shore
simply a noise we cannot hear, a hundred yards into
the distant blur.

*Think of it: not only were we moving toward the light,
we were becoming light.*

We always knew that if we wanted to knit anything we
could have gotten all the wool we'd ever need from him. If
we had wanted to, we could have knit eternally, there was
no end to the amount of wool we could've had.

What we got was one paperbag filled with a
few charcoal-grey skeins—I had picked out the color, it
was to be a sweater for me, my mother was going to
knit it.

Then, for years, we moved this paperbag around
the house, trying to find a place for it, somewhere that
would insist. It was on the list of projects, but it was a
project forever delayed.

*No sense in knitting something you will outgrow in a
year,* she'd say.

Before there were fields there was ocean. It covered the
fields and what drowned inside it became earth. Before
there were oceans there were stars, one exploded and
the oceans rained down. Before sheep there were wild
sheep, they lived in the forests, the men came and captured
them, their fleece so matted, it grew so long it dragged
on the earth, thick with brambles. Men invented knives
to shear them, invented the comb to brush it out, let the
sheep run naked through the fields, which had been coral
gardens a million years before . . .

I ask my daughter what she was before she was born
and she says, *Nothing, I wasn't anything before thi*s.

My mother's side of the family came over from England
to Massachusetts in the mid-1800s and opened a wool mill
in Canton. If you go to Canton today, the name Draper
is still on many buildings, there is still a Draper mill,
though this might be other, more distant relatives. I don't
know the exact genealogy, nor do I much care. If you
go inside you will find machines, looms, invented by my
relatives, distant or otherwise, the name Draper stamped
onto each one. But by the time I knew my grandfather
the bottom of the wool market had fallen out. When I'd
go to his office he'd be at his desk, looking into a blank
screen. He'd be on the phone, talking to another old guy,
a crony from the day. *Five hundred skeins of Wyoming
grade A mohair top,* and the crony would take it off his
hands. On the walls of his office were etchings of sheep,
Currier & Ives, men with tops hats lining the pens.
This was the world, and then it changed. In this way all
the money passed down from all those wars slipped
through his hands and flowed out the hole in the bottom.

This is the truth about the war: my grandfather came
from money, and so he would never see combat—he was
a Seabee, construction brigade. His job was to supply
the ships with food, with clothes. His war was far from the
bombs, from the fires, from the blur. He wasn't at
Normandy, he did not storm the beach, he did not run
into the fire.

And so he came home from his war, intact (mostly),
and there was his daughter, now almost six, her hand
still so tiny in his. Remember: before she defied him,
before she brought shame, before she went off with one
of the men who dug ditches in town, she was a child.
Then, just as my grandfather was leaving his wife for his
secretary at the Top Company (*meet me in Reno, love,
and we will begin our new life*), his daughter got pregnant.
Years later, when I am twelve, she will take another
man's name (the Vietnam vet), which leaves us, her and
I, with different names. Then, four years later, when
he finally leaves, she will go back to her father's name,
her maiden name, but even this will not be back far
enough. One day she will take one more step back, to
a time before she was born. As if Penelope, by her
unweaving, finally reduced—returned—the tapestry
back into a few skeins of wool.

If it had been possible to put the wool back onto
the sheep I believe my mother would have done it.

The wool waited for years in its paperbag. Two red needles
poking out of the top. My grandfather would ask about
it, at our monthly lunches in his mansion, the mansion
he inherited from his father. My mother needed to make
something with what she'd been given, before she'd be
given anything more.

Currier & Ives on the walls.

A bookcase lined with porcelain sheep.

A wine cellar.

Six crackers on a plate, enough for two apiece.

I'd wear one of the plaid Pendleton shirts my
grandfather gave me for Christmas each year.

That way he wouldn't even have to touch it to know
it was pure.

But still, he touched it.

my mother, outside her father's house on first cliff (is she giving my brother a sip of beer?), scituate, ma, 1960

At one point my mother picked up the blood red needles and began, she must have taught herself. I can remember the sweater, I wore it constantly—charcoal gray, cable knit on the front—but I cannot see her sitting still long enough to make it. I cannot remember when it was new, but I remember the end of it, the elbows, blown out from wear. By the end it was simply, again, little more than a pile of yarn. One sweater, out of all those sheep, all that wool, all those factories, all those looms.

    After the elbows were blown out I put it in mothballs and pulled it out only for our monthly lunches, which, near the end, were more like every other month, if that. Cables on the front, the sleeves too long, knit from wool he'd graded himself on a ranch I never saw in Montana—this was the uniform I wore to his house, until the end. That mothball chemical smell hung off me as I sat in the mansion—could everyone smell it or just me? By then I was drinking and once he even offered me a beer, but I didn't stop at one. *Look at what I have made*, my mother might have uttered, *from the scraps you have offered.*

from *this is the night our house will catch fire*

ON THRESHOLDS

The idea that writing can give meaning to chaos—
I don't know if that's true. At the moment, for
me, that seems like an attempt to exert too much
control over this enormous and incomprehensible
world. It seems there's always another threshold
to cross, which might simply be part of the beauty
and the terror of getting older. I hear myself say,
oh yeah, I've already dealt with that thing, that night
our house caught fire, say, but then something
rises up and forces me to realize that I haven't dealt
with it much at all. Right now, I'm pretty sure I'm at
the end of something, that I've come into the last
psychic space that's unexplored, but that's bullshit.
In ten years I'm pretty sure I'll think, *my god,
I thought that was it?*

jacquelyn gallo & casey haymes
talk with nick flynn, *12th street journal*,
the new school, 2016

RED SOX

(1975) A helicopter lifts out of the embassy, people cling
to the landing struts, we see some fall. This is how the
undeclared war ends. Her second husband, Travis, moves
out as we watch the helicopters on the evening news.
Shortly thereafter my mother, brother and I begin a
summer of watching baseball on television. That we hadn't
given a damn about the Red Sox until then, not really,
doesn't matter. We need to toughen up.

That summer she cuts off all her hair, becomes
a vegetarian, and drops way too much weight, to hover
in the ghostly realm, the realm of vapor and shade.
Hollow-eyed, spooked. My brother sits down to dinner
with her, shovels in the offered vegetables and grains,
but I'm annoyed I have to buy my own meat. By now she's
taking pills for her migraines, pills to wake up. Thirty-
five and her second marriage has ended as badly as the
first. To me Travis had been a reckless older buddy, scary-
fun. As a husband he'd been a nightmare. After two
years in Vietnam he'd barely fit into our mickey-mouse
cottage, our badly converted summer shack. They were
together from the time I was eleven until I was fifteen,
and each year he lived with us our house felt smaller and
smaller, in spite of the additions. They slept together
for the first couple years in the room he'd built, then he
began sleeping on a cot set up in that same room, then
he began sleeping at a house he was renovating, unrolling
his Marine sleeping bag on the floor of the job site. Then
he was gone.

The Red Sox started out that spring bristling with
promise, but everyone knew they would break our hearts.
Don't get too excited, it's not going to last—this is the mantra
of the Red Sox fan, the mantra of our Irish Catholic
town. Don't hope for much in this life and you won't be
disappointed. Save hope for the afterlife.

That spring into summer Travis would return,
unannounced, take something he'd left behind—his
primer-coated MG from the driveway; a photograph of
a mountain from the bedroom, laminated onto a board
he'd "distressed" with a blowtorch and a hammer. Slowly
he emptied the garage of broken skilsaws and pornography,
leaving behind half-filled cans of paint. Unnerving, his
presence still thick around us, my mother would look up

from dinner and ask, *Where're the wineglasses?* and we'd know
he'd been standing in that spot by the shelf just hours
before, when the house was empty for the day. Since he'd
done the renovations it was useless to try to lock him out—
the windows all salvaged, lockless.

Part of watching the Red Sox together was to hunker
down, circle the wagons, show a unified front. Travis kept
coming back and we needed to fortify against him. But
the greater (if unspoken) part for my brother and me was
to be close to our mother, to keep an eye on her. It was
clear she was slipping away from us, from this world. My
brother understood this first, I think, or I just didn't want
to understand it. We'd huddle in her bedroom, transfixed,
as men who had a clear sense of purpose strode up to the
plate to face down our newfound heroes. Bill "Spaceman"
Lee—who advocated the reform of marijuana laws and
had spoken out against the war in Vietnam. Luis Tiante—
the overweight Cuban exile—whose tics and gestures
were weirder than those of any human being we'd ever
seen. His mid-windup pivot could last so long that it was
impossible to hold your breath while he stared into the
infield. He waggled and ducked and twisted and toppled
and sneered and menaced and paused and, as one
commentator noticed, looked like he was trying to kick
off his left shoe. There was something about his body,
how all of this struggle led to so many perfect throws,
that gave us hope. He didn't make it look easy.
    I'm fifteen, an age when most kids are breaking
from their parents, spending more time with their friends,
developing a secret language only they can understand.
But now my mother, brother and I are developing our own
common language, talking about Fred Lynn and Bernie
Carbo over dinner, over our newfound couscous and
curries. We know the strengths and weaknesses of each
player, how they'd done against the A's last time around,
who to watch out for, who was a hitter, who'd made
what incredible catch. I'd been raised to be independent,
cooked for myself since I could reach the stove, never had
an allowance, left to my own bad devices for as long as
memory. My mother had made it clear that she wouldn't
be around forever—*If something happens to me . . .* , she'd say.
To look into her face for too long only brought up dread.
To stare as one into the television on a hot Saturday

afternoon, to glimpse the world outside still going on, unfolding with or without us, to feel part of something larger, something that made it into the newspapers every day, that people seemed excited about, something to get caught up in and carried along by—Tiante would be pitching next Saturday, maybe reason enough to stick around, if just to see how it turned out, if just to see him smoke the bastards.

Then the improbable happened—the Red Sox kept winning. Carlton Fisk stood at the plate and the entire Eastern Seaboard held its breath. A big man, "Pudge" leaned into his swing, effortlessly he could knock it out of the park, we'd seen it before, it was in him. We didn't breathe.

In the end they broke our hearts, but not before getting us almost to Thanksgiving. Sprawled in her bedroom, my mother propped up with pillows, I'm on my belly beside her, my brother in the la-z-boy. It's all history now, something about the sixth game of the Series against the Reds, how Pudge hammers one at the last possible moment, bottom of the twelfth, how it hangs over the foul line for an eternity, how he stops halfway to first and jumps in the air, swinging his arms to the right to force it fair. I remember perfectly, the way his body moved, jumping up on his toes, a series of little bunny-hops, his big hands pushing the air like a desperate Zeus, how everyone at the game or watching on tv does the same, damn near screams, *Come on*, it's that important, to win this one game, to let us all move to the next.

from *another bullshit night in suck city*

mark adams, *a field guide to getting lost*
(an activation of *The Ticking Is the Bomb*), 2017

a field guide to getting lost

Here's a secret: Everyone, if they live long enough, will lose their way at some point. You will lose your way, you will wake up one morning and find yourself lost. This is a hard, simple truth. If it hasn't happened to you yet consider yourself lucky. When it does, when one day you look around and nothing is recognizable, when you find yourself alone in a dark wood having lost the way, you may find it easier to blame someone else—an errant lover, a missing father, a bad childhood. Or it may be easier to blame the map you were given—folded too many times, out of date, tiny print. You can shake your fist at the sky, call it *fate*, *karma*, *bad luck*, and sometimes it is. But, for the most part, if you are honest, you will only be able to blame yourself. Life can, of course, blindside you, yet often as not we choose to be blind—*agency*, some call it. If you're lucky you'll remember a story you heard as a child, the trick of leaving a trail of breadcrumbs, the idea being that after whatever it is that is going to happen in those woods has happened, you can then retrace your steps, find your way back out. But no one said you wouldn't be changed, by the hours, the years, spent wandering those woods.

SUDDEN

If it had been a heart attack, the newspaper
might have used the word *massive*,
    as if a mountain range had opened
    inside her, but instead

it used the word *suddenly*, a light coming on

in an empty room. The telephone

fell from my shoulder, a black parrot repeating
        something happened, something awful

a sunday, dusky. If it had been

terminal, we could have cradled her
as she grew smaller, wiped her mouth,

        said good-bye. But it was *sudden*

how overnight we could be orphaned
& the world become a bell we'd crawl inside
& the ringing all we'd eat.

from *some ether*

ON PURCHASE

In my first book I had a poem coming
from my mother's point of view, and
a poem coming from the bullet's point
of view. I was trying to take different
routes up the mountain, attempting   .
to find different purchase on the
material. *Purchase*—so many ways up
that mountain feel uncomfortable,
but I've come to trust that discomfort
is a dowsing rod for where the water
is. It's like in a dream where something
bad is happening behind a door. You
have the choice to either turn away
or to open the door. And it seems for
poets, or for any artist, or maybe
for any human being, it just seems like
maybe you should open the door.
But you should only open it when you're
able to. You might not be in shape,
at that moment—psychically, spiritually,
whatever—to open the door. You
might need a few years of whatever it
is you do to make yourself healthy
before you're able to open that door.
You might have to leave the door closed
for a while, which I think is a perfectly
valid choice.

kaveh akbar talks with nick flynn,
divedapper, 2017

nick flynn, *ten fingers*, 2012

FIORINAL

In *Magnolia*, Julianne Moore enters a drugstore to fill a prescription, ostensibly for her husband, who is dying of cancer, but the pharmacist thinks she is trying to scam him for drugs. He thinks she's an addict, or maybe her character just thinks he thinks this, it's unclear. It seems like she might be scamming, or at least taking a swig of the liquid morphine now and then, or perhaps she is simply distraught, to be so close to death; either way, she goes off on him, in a way that is chilling and complicated, because no one seems to know at that moment what is real. If Julianne, looking for her *motivation*, asked her director, *Am I trying to scam the drugs or am I distraught?* perhaps the director simply shrugged—all possible scenarios are sometimes true.

nick flynn, *yojimbo*, 2011

(2011) I'm on the phone with Julianne, a month before we start filming, we're on speakerphone with Paul. They are, well, I don't know where they are—I imagine a hotel room, maybe a restaurant—just voices without bodies, asking questions about my mother. I say hi to Julianne, say how happy I am she is involved, that I look forward to meeting her. Paul asks, Do you have time to talk? I'm outside a bike shop, about to buy a bike (mine was recently stolen)—I have time. So your mother shot herself? he asks. I didn't just make that up, did I? No, you didn't make that up. Where'd she get the gun? he asks. We had lots of guns around my house, I tell him. Some antique ones hung on the wall, a working shotgun in a zippered bag in the closet, the shells in my mother's top drawer. I'd sometimes put them into the gun when she wasn't around, but I don't tell Paul this, nor do I tell Julianne. I don't know why I don't tell them—maybe because my mother didn't know (at least I thought she didn't know), so Julianne doesn't need to know (or maybe she knows already). I tell them she had her own pistol, a .38, which she got a permit for in 1972. I would go target shooting with her, and then later I'd shoot a rifle with my stepfather, the Vietnam vet, and then some other guns with my friends, who were into guns—guns, motorcycles, and beer (and

Mink DeVille). I liked the motorcycles and the beer (and Mink DeVille), though I wasn't that into the guns. I tell them that after she died the cops came and took all the guns away, confiscated them. That I never went to retrieve them.

nick flynn, *good bad ugly,* 2004

On the phone Julianne asks, though it is hard for me to hear, about pills: Which pills did your mother take? I tell her about the Darvon, which I don't even know if they still make, but I believe it was a barbiturate—a knockout pill, a down—she took them for her migraines. Julianne says, O, my mother had migraines too, and I say, O. How old was your mother when she had you? Julianne asks, and I say she was twenty, twenty-one, and Julianne says, My mother was twenty when she had me, and I say, O, yes, so you know, but even as I say the words I don't know what they mean. She asks about her depression and I say, It was mostly just when she had migraines that she'd go inside, that she'd spend a day in bed, that other than that she was vivacious, young, alive. She made it to work every day, and then she went to her other job at night. She didn't miss work, until maybe near the end, when she started doing cocaine and things got a little sloppy. Everyone was doing cocaine then, I add, and Julianne laughs. She got a little off the rails but not so far off. I am leaning over a wrought-iron railing, looking into a restaurant—a Chinese man comes to the window, looks up at me.

Paul plans Julianne's scenes—which are all flashback—to
be filmed in such a way that they appear washed out,
faded, yellowed. Your mother is the specter hanging over
every scene, Paul tells me—her presence, her death, is
what animates the living.
Does that sound right? he asks.

What I don't tell Julianne is this: I remember a lot of
orange pill bottles around our house, my mother would
save them, perhaps to get them refilled, perhaps to keep
track, her top drawer rattled with them. Behind the pill
bottles was her gun, alongside a copy of Henry Miller,
Sexus, The Rosy Crucifixion—this was the drawer where
the action was. At some point, when I was around Liam's
age, I began taking the pill bottles, stuffing them with
firecrackers. I'd cut a little hole into the white childproof
caps with an x-acto knife, run the braided fuses through
it, to make my little bombs. I would aim the gun out
the window at passing cars, *bang*, I'd make the noise with
my mouth. I'd thumb through the Miller and jerk off.
Later still I'd simply take the pills themselves, *to see how
far they could take me.*

Julianne is now in the bathroom. Paul comes up as I watch
the screen, but all I can see is the way the light is caught
on the tiles behind her. Julianne simply sits there, on the
toilet, her painkillers balanced on the sink beside her.
She stares at the orange pill bottle, she must have stared at
it, before she struggled off the childproof cap, before she
dumped out the white capsules, before she put them inside
her. A month ago, on the phone I'd told Julianne that my
mother took Darvon for her headaches. Today she told me
that her mother would take Fiorinal—Yes, that's it, that's
what she took, I'd forgotten the word (maybe she took both—
she took a lot).
Fiorinal—it sounds like a species of orchid.
It sounds like a Glass Flower we forgot to make.
ACTION.
Julianne looks away from the pill bottle first, looks
at something outside the frame, avoiding the pills, for a
while. I lean over, past Paul, to see into the screen, and
I get a whiff of stale beer—three glasses on the table half-
filled with beer. Props? Why use real beer? A cuckoo clock
calls out. Is the cuckoo clock real?

I never went to the police station to retrieve my mother's guns—for all I know, they are still locked in a room somewhere. Or else one day they were auctioned off. Or else they simply vanished. Maybe someone uses one of them every year (the shotgun) to shoot a deer, to feed his family, or maybe someone used another one, the same gun my mother used (the .38), to end his (or her) life. Maybe I should have retrieved them, melted them down, I could have forged them into something—an urn, something big enough to sleep in, *and the ringing become a bell we'd crawl inside / and the sound is all we'd eat.*

from *the reenactments*

I was vapor, I was air, I was nowhere.

rebecca keith talks with nick flynn,
the millions, 2010

rachel eliza griffiths, *black music box
with white room*, 2015

AMANUENSIS

If you write about painting
yourself into a

corner (*I have lived so much
with you not being here*)

then you might find yourself, in
fact, one

day, painted
into a corner. Or you might find

yourself on the edge of

a cliff, or maybe facedown on
the carpet in a white

white room. Why not, then, try
to write yourself out, into a

field, say, or

onto a country road, or
kneedeep in a river that might or

must open into the sea—if you
write it out the words could become

clear, not blurry, no, like

that photograph of your mother—
calm, looking straight

into the you you are now

as she holds on to the you you were
as you both play-struggle

against her . . .

from *I will destroy you*

AS WE DRIVE SLOWLY PAST THE BURNING HOUSE

(1971) When a siren—police car or fire truck or ambulance—
punctured my Saturday morning cartoons, twisting the
blue from the sky, my mother would tell me to go start the
car. *Let's see what's happening*, she'd say, and we'd drive, to
the place where the sirens called us. Afterward we'd drive
to the coffee shop in the harbor and I'd go in and order
her the usual—*cream no sugar*—while she'd wait in the car.
She'd worked in that same coffee shop when she was in high
school—it was where she met my father. *I don't want to
give them anything more to talk about*, she'd once told me, to
explain why she'd send me in alone.

    After I'd come back with her coffee, we'd drive to
the beach, sit in the car, look out at the Atlantic. One day
she told me that she was thinking of marrying a carpenter
she'd been seeing for a couple months. *Travis wants me to
marry him*, she said. *What do you think?* Travis was just back
from Vietnam—ten years younger than her, ten years older
than me (I'm eleven)—a nice enough guy, but a little wild.

    That's a mistake, I tell her.

    A couple weeks later Travis is living in our house.

    After they're married my mother and I still drive
toward our burning houses. Travis never joins us—maybe
he's never invited. Once we drove past the house of a
woman who'd killed herself—no siren had announced
it. Maybe we read about it in the paper, maybe we heard
about it from a neighbor, but still we got in the car, and
drove slowly past. It was a house I'd never noticed, though
I'd passed by it every morning on my paper route, the
windows now curtained shut, the grass already overgrown.

    As we drove slowly past our burning houses, what
was my mother hoping to find, what was she hoping I'd
see? Was she hoping to teach me to pay close attention to
the world? Or close attention to the afterworld? In *The
Odyssey* the sirens sang out to Odysseus to lull him into
stranding his ship on the shoals—it could be argued that
our sirens were merely calling out to strand us as well, to
scuttle our ship, only it would take years to know that was
what they were doing. Or, it could be argued, at least it
wasn't our tragedy, at least we were able to step outside our
house for an hour, into the fresh air, to witness something
outside ourselves. To empathize, or to practice empathy,
even though we never knew the people who'd lived in the

burning houses, nor did it seem we cared to, even after their house was gone. What could we have possibly offered—a room in our falling-down house? (*There was no room.*) A meal, a blanket, some clothes? (*We never did.*)

Or maybe my mother simply wanted me to practice, like other families practiced fire drills, so that when the sirens came for her I'd know what to do. To get in the car and drive, toward the sound, whatever it was—fire or heart attack, car crash or suicide—to get out and stand on the sidewalk or on someone's lawn. Or to not even stop, to make it a slow drive-by, while the stranger is carried away on a stretcher. Maybe she believed she could tell by looking everyone in the eye as they came out of the house if it was a scam or not. Or maybe she just wanted to make sure all the children made it out okay. But where do you drive to when the siren is outside your own house? What do you look at when the strangers on the sidewalk are looking at you?

from *The Ticking Is the Bomb*

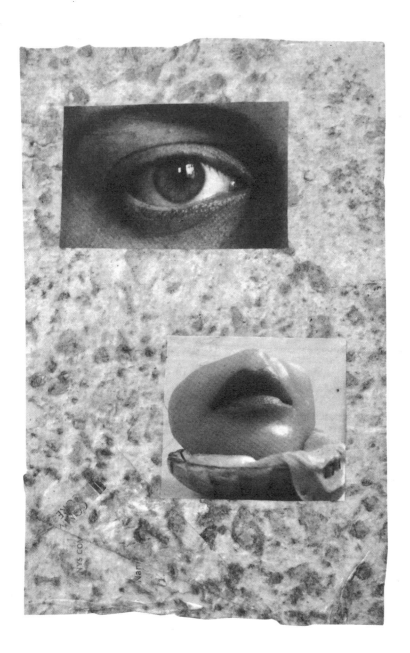

nick flynn, *eye, mouth*, 2015

ATLANTIC CITY

We took a road trip, less than a month after my mother
killed herself, my girlfriend and I. We got a *Drive-Away*
car—the deal was you were given a car to drive across
the country or wherever on the promise you would
deliver it to someone at the other end—do they still
do that? Seems unlikely. My girlfriend and I hitchhiked
up to a car dealership in New Hampshire and were
given the keys to a brand-new BMW. We drove it from
New Hampshire to Florida, and on the way, we lived
in it. We slept in it, we ate in it, we fucked in it. And we
listened to the radio, because back then that's what you
did. One song was very popular at that moment, a strange
song, really, it seemed, for Top Ten radio, but I would
look forward to it, and turn it up, whenever it came on.
It was Springsteen's "Atlantic City," from *Nebraska*
(as a cassette tape of it, as it seems unlikely I would have
heard that song so many times in so many states . . .).
Either way, this is the song I remember listening to,
that I looked forward to hearing, in those dark days. I
would like to say they were darkest of my life, but that
wouldn't be true. With her death, it was as if something
had happened to me, but in the years to follow I would
become the agent of my own harm. In the immediate
aftermath the pull within me to follow her down was
strong. It would be strong at other times in my life, but
more subtly so. Can I say that in the years since never
did I come quite so close to the edge? Doubtful.

> *Everything dies baby that's a fact*
> *Maybe everything that dies some day comes back.*

These were the lines that got me, biblical in their
promise, a prophecy speaking to me directly, at that
moment. It was always speaking to me, all down
the Eastern Seaboard.

We used maps, we listened to the radio, we used
payphones.

At one point, in Georgia, sometime after midnight,
we drove slowly past a Cadillac burning. It appeared to
be set, and recently, as the flames reached above our heads.

There was, seemingly, no one else for miles ahead of us, or behind us, or anywhere near that flaming car.

The song that was playing, as we drove slowly past, was "Atlantic City." This was always the song that was playing.

Maybe everything that dies some day comes back.

I would usually cry when I heard that line. I wouldn't let my girlfriend see me cry, though if you ask her about it now she might say I was crying all the time, though I don't know why she would have let me drive if that were true, and I definitely drove.

It was winter break. My mother had died a couple weeks before Christmas. I would end up dropping out of college the following spring, though at the time I was trying to hold it together, whatever that might mean. A road trip seemed like a good idea. Or at least an idea.

Maybe one needs to be young to be saved by a song, by a piece of art, to allow oneself to be so fully invested in something outside yourself. I could say that my girlfriend saved my life as much as Bruce Springsteen. I could say that driving a BMW, that perfect machine, saved my life.

I could say that the way it would rain every afternoon in Key West, I could say the rooming house we found, I could say the way everyone would stand at sunset and applaud the sun the moment it touched the sea. *Maybe everything that dies some day comes back.* I could hear that the narrator of the song didn't really believe that, that it was what he needed to say at that moment. I knew that nothing comes back, but him saying it, singing it, brought me something like peace, or at least release. Tears.

I cannot say that at some point on the trip to Key West that I had an epiphany, an *I want to live* moment. I cannot say I didn't sneer at the tourists lined up on the pier and applauding each night when the sun went down. I would muddle through the years after that, years where it felt like I was wading through molasses. I would come to hate Springsteen and his false promises, I would purge my record collection of all his albums, and then I would come

around to him again, years later, and listen to the story of
the small-time hood that somehow got me to the other side.

Maybe it was the confusion I heard in Springsteen's lyric,
the false bravado, of an artist willing to exist in a messy
state, in a lie, that saved me. Self-help books never did
much for me, but if I could hear another human being
calling out from the wilderness then I knew that at least
I was still among the living, which was all I could hope for
at that moment.

from a public talk for the lecture series
arts in mind—the topic was "this piece saved
my life"—curated by joshua wolf shenk,
the new school, 2012

UNKNOWN

Phone rings—UNKNOWN
again—mom

again, but I'm not
answering. I'd email her

a photo of her grandchild
but her account is dead,

besides, she

doesn't have a computer. Or
a smart phone. Or

eyes. Or hands. How

does she speak without a mouth,
how does she dial without

fingers? How many words are

still inside her, trapped now
forever—is she still like a pencil,

full of words, or is she no longer
like a pencil?

from *I will destroy you*

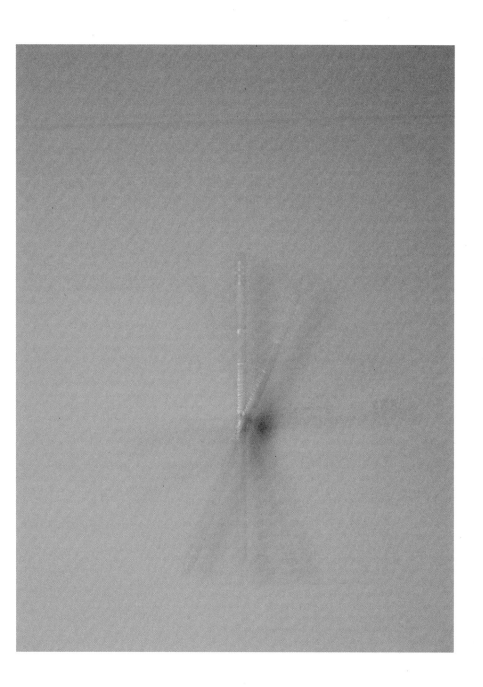

catherine opie, *for unknown*, 2016

ON CHAOS

Perhaps I have a high tolerance for
chaos, or for at least trying to find
a way to sit quietly in the midst of
it. When I'm in the midst of a longer
project it can seem that everywhere
I turn a piece of the puzzle is waiting
for me, and my job is to simply gather
these pieces together. I do this in
notebooks, mostly, and then as they
make their way into my computer
I begin the process of distilling them
down, to find an essence, a pattern.

Adrienne Rich offers this:

Once you live any piece of your vision
it opens you to a constant onslaught.
Of necessities, of horrors, but of wonders,
too, of possibilities . . . like meteor
showers all the time, bombardment,
constant connections.

Can it be that simple, that to live any
piece of your vision you can reach a
place where the ego might dissolve into
the meteor shower . . . ?

sarah anne johnson talks with nick flynn,
the writer's chronicle, 2015

mom & me, brook street, 1965

CANOPIC

One summer night our house catches fire. I'm six. I run
through the smoke to escape the flames . . . A thousand
and one times I've told this story. *Why?* Because
it happened. Because I escaped. Because it involves
fire, and firemen, and sirens. Because it's what
everyone fears, and here I am—I stand before you,
seemingly intact.

Sometimes still this story starts with just me,
barefoot in the next-door neighbor's yard, looking
back at the house we've just tumbled out of—all I
can do now is watch as it burns. By way of comfort,
Didion offers this:

> *. . . we have to learn to freeze the shifting*
> *phantasmagoria which is our actual experience . . .*

Phantasmagoria—I need to freeze—make sense
of—the story of being six and running through a
burning house. I needed to contain it, like a firefly
in a jar. If I don't contain it I don't know if I can
move away from it, and if I can't move away from
it I don't know if I'll ever believe that I made it out
in one piece.

> *Here I am. I stand before you. Intact.*
> *Whole. Holy.*
> *Everything that lives is holy.*

What was it we used to chant into the mirror
every morning, in what used to be called "The New
Age"? *Every day, in every way, getting better & better.*
What is it we chant now? Eduardo Corral offers this:

> *Some days, when I catch my*
> *reflection in a mirror,*
> *I think, Someone has hurt this animal . . .*

It was a perfect summer day, Mom's boyfriend
(let's call him Vernon) grilled hamburgers on the
back deck. Then, after we'd all gone off to bed, after
Mom (I guess) tucked me in, raccoons came and

knocked over the hibachi and the coals fanned out
across the wooden planks.

It was then only a matter of time.

But it was always a story, like all stories, that
came in several jars, like those jars the Egyptians
would use to hold the entrails of their dead—
canopic—lungs in one, spleen in another, liver in
one, heart in another. You've seen these jars—empty
now, the heart long desiccated—in the Egyptian
wing of the Brooklyn Museum.

Years later, when asked about my childhood,
I'll say, *It was happy*—for years after the fire
this is the only jar I'll ever open. *THE HAPPY
JAR*. If you happen to know about my mother and
how she died, the next question is often, *How
did you survive?* meaning, *How the hell are you
so well-adjusted?* Well-adjusted? I'll think to myself,
but I'll answer, as I always answer, *I felt love,
I knew my mother loved me.*

I'll answer this way even after (*shifting
phantasmagoria*) I learn that she'd set the fire herself.

I'm thirty-five when I track down Vernon.
Thirty-five is (perhaps) the age when one can
approach the past without believing it will annihilate
you. To annihilate means to reduce to nothing.
To ash. Vernon laughs when I mention the raccoons.
That house was a real shithole, he says, *all it needed
was a match*. He tells me she had something going
on with the local insurance agent, that she got the
house insured for more than it was worth. As he
speaks I both know & don't know what that means.
In that moment one jar became two. In one was
the fire, in the other was my mother setting the
fire. In one I was happy, in one I'd survived, in the
other I never made it out of that house. One meant
my mother was clever, resourceful, that she knew
how to get over. One meant she was broke, it meant
we would get a nicer house, and we did. The other
meant something else, something I wasn't ready

to take in, not fully—it's entirely possible I'm still
not ready, but here I am.

Whole. Holy. Full of holes.

Afterwards, smoke becomes my dreams—I
can breathe in it. Afterwards, the bedroom, all
bedrooms, are thick with smoke. Afterwards, smoke
tastes good inside me, smoke is a blanket, smoke
asks a question, and the question is (always) *Why not?*

Afterwards, if asked, I'll tell you that it's
possible—likely—that my mother set our house
on fire with me asleep inside it, and the worst thing
about it is that I'll tell you all this with a smile.

Here's a line from a poem I wrote before
I knew she'd set it—*You can always run back into a
burning house* . . .

If not for the child sleeping upstairs then the
fireman, the insurance man, the policeman, all might
ask questions. The child had to be asleep upstairs
to make the scam believable. This is the jar you put it
into, after you heard it was she who lit the match.
It was the jar labeled, *MY MOTHER KNEW HOW
TO STICK IT TO THE MAN*. She put a roof over our
heads, even if—even as—she burned it down.

First there was one jar, then two, then
many—as a story it began to multiply.

In this jar is a plan—the plan is that the firemen
will come in time. Only they didn't come in time—
she had to make her way through the now burning
house to your bed, shake you from your dream
of smoke. You were a fish gasping for water on a tile
floor, you were inside a balloon (*balloon rhymes with
raccoon*) rising from a child's fist, you were the endless
inside of the vacuum cleaner and the memory of
how it smells.

QUESTION:
Did she really have a plan? Was it always the plan to
save you? Was she always going to wake you with a
word—*RUN*—or did the word find her?

QUESTION:
Why do you think she bought a house across from a
fire station?

QUESTION:
Which came first, the fire or the idea of the fire?
The sound of the alarm or the alarm itself? Think
of the power contained in one match, the power
to go back to before there are children. She is still
young, she could start again. She lights the first
match and knows they will come—one match can
make the whole station light up with sirens.

QUESTION:
What if the word *RUN* was only in her head?

In the years after the fire—*seven, eight, nine*—
you watch her, as she twirls her hair obsessively,
driving to another somewhere with you in the car
beside her. Ten years later she'll be in a strip club
snorting coke with her gangster boyfriend. Five
years after that she'll be dead. She'll make a hole
in the fabric of the universe but this time she won't
try to push you through it, this time she'll leave you
alone on this side of it.

In this jar you sit on the bank of a brook, you
see the water for what it is, made of a thousand suns.
You could have sat there forever, you could have died
on that bank (clearly, part of you has). In the death
dream you swear it was enough, that your life had
been full, happy, instead of waking up at three a.m.
unable to remember where you are or who is beside
you. Instead of waking up unable to breathe (*hello
married life*). You've been dreaming about a river,
about a stick, about a boy who knew he was loved, a
boy who kept pulling the stick in & out of the water,
a boy who knew what he could do & couldn't do
with everything. It is so simple, yet why can't you

breathe? You might as well simply write about the
stick, if that is all you have, or the brook, as you
press your stick into it, as you watch the water find
its way around it, almost at once.

Here I am. Whole. Holy. When I tell my
daughter about the fire she looks at the sun. I don't
tell her that my mother—her grandmother—
set it, just as when she asks how she died, I don't
tell her about the gun. I simply say, *She had a bad
heart*—this is the only jar I offer. Love, if you are
reading this now, I'm sorry I lied to you—you
were only seven, I didn't want you to know, before
you had even fully landed on this planet, that
your grandmother had chosen to leave it. I didn't
want you to know that it was an option, that it
was something in our blood. I didn't want you
to know that at one point, when I was your age,
she might have considered, with one match,
to simply fold me—us—back into the universe.

from *this is the night our house will catch fire*

nick flynn, *jellyfish*, 2003

HIVE

What would you do inside me?
You would be utterly

lost, labyrinthine

comb, each corridor identical, a
funhouse, *there*, a bridge, worker

knit to worker, a span
you can't cross. On the other side

the queen, a fortune of honey.

Once we filled an entire house with it,
built the comb between floorboard

& joist, slowly at first, the constant

buzz kept the owners awake, then
louder, until honey began to seep

from the walls, swell
the doorframes. Our gift.

They had to burn the house down
to rid us.

from *blind huber*

my mother (before she was my mother),
scituate, ma, 1947

GIDDY-UP

My grandfather, my mother's father, calls in the Irish girl who takes care of him by ringing a small brass bell, which is shaped like a crane. I am visiting him a few weeks before my daughter is born. He holds the bell by its beak as he shakes it. If I let myself imagine what I would like to have to remember him by, all I can imagine is this bell, this crane. Framed on the wall behind his head is a silhouette, I remember my mother making it during a blackout, my brother aiming a flashlight at my head, my mother tracing my profile with a pencil onto the black paper tacked to the wall. I remember her taking it down, then cutting it out. The Irish girl comes in, smiles, leans over the bed, asks, *And what can I do for you now*, her blond pigtails nearly brushing his face, but already he has closed his eyes again. As a girl my mother wore her hair in pigtails, I have pictures, I've seen the painting of her beside the horse. I even remember her in pigtails, sometimes, when she was my mother. Strange, but in my grandfather's room, in his whole house, there are no photographs of her. It's not that it's a house without photographs—walls, bookcases, tabletops, all sit thick with cousins, uncles, strangers— photographs are everywhere. But none of my mother, and as for my brother and I, only this one silhouette—it's as if our branch had been erased and was now merely a shadow. Grandpa and I never talk about my mother, not really, but I interviewed him once about her, when I made the documentary, the home movie, about her ex-boyfriends.

I wanted to ask him one of the questions I'd asked each of them— *How did you find out she'd died?* Grandpa wore a suit for the interview, sat upright behind his desk, but seconds into it he began crying—I'd never seen him cry before. *I didn't know how to help her*, he said. Ten years later, ten more years of not uttering her name, and I've been sitting with him when I can, since he broke his hip. Sometimes he talks to me about the universe, sometimes about his fever dreams, and sometimes I transcribe what he says in a small notebook. Both of us know that this bed is his deathbed—he will die two days after Maeve is born, he will never hold her. The Irish girl and I are with him now. He opens his eyes, tells us his dream—*I was walking down a mountain road, and a man approached me in a carriage, drawn by four horses. The carriage stopped beside me, the man opened the door, but I said I'd rather walk.* He smiles, then he closes his eyes. The Irish girl winks at me, leans over him, asks again what she can do for him. He opens his eyes, takes a pigtail in each of his hands— *Giddy-up*, he says.

from *The Ticking Is the Bomb*

LAST KISS

The Queen, asleep in the forest, her body laid out on a stone slab. Moonlight on her cheek, the blanket that covers her is blood-red. A willow weaves a mottled canopy of dark above her.

This, like many fairy tales, centers on a kiss.

If the Prince finds her in time he can wake her, but he is unsure which path to take—maybe the ravens have (once again) eaten the breadcrumbs. If he gets there too late she will never wake up.

The moral, if there is one, is that there really is no way to know when something—anything—that you do every day, or even something you've done only once, will turn out to be the last time. The cup you drink your coffee from each morning—your favorite cup—is already broken. If you can think of the cup this way then you will, perhaps, hold on to it more tightly. Perhaps you will appreciate each moment you still have with it until it does, finally, forever, break.

Everything is already broken.

The kiss that comes to mind, if asked, is the last kiss I gave my mother—it rises up, unbidden. It's dusk, she's upstairs, lying in her bed, coming out of—or going into—another migraine. It's just after Thanksgiving, I've come home for a few days for the holiday. I'm living outside of the house by now, finishing up my junior year at college. My mother is still young—forty-two, still beautiful, still desired—young enough to start over. Her boyfriend's been in jail for a couple years now (he got caught smuggling drugs). He's up for parole in a month, but while he's been away she's been seeing someone else. I've been out with friends, likely getting high in our cars in the Peggotty Beach parking lot—these days I am always getting high. I'm home now to say goodbye, to let her know I'm about to get on my motorcycle and push on, ride back up to school. I climb the stairs to her bedroom. The lights are off, a tiny orange bottle of white pills within reach. Her eyes are closed, her blanket is red, her skin alabaster—maybe she's a little high herself, or a little hungover. The Queen is in pain, maybe mortal pain. If she doesn't open her eyes she might never open them, the Prince knows this, he's been wandering this forest his whole life, the breadcrumbs all eaten. The Prince leans over her face, as he had done so many times, to whisper the words that will keep her there, only the words don't come, or they come out wrong. *Can I get you anything?* The voice coming out of him (*see you soon*) doesn't even sound like him. *Kiss her*, it murmurs, & so he does & her eyes open & the spell, for that brief moment, is broken.

from *this is the night our house will catch fire*

nick flynn, *laundry* (julianne moore on set
of *being flynn*), 2011

DISSOLVE

After eight takes it all dissolves—I look at the screen and
it isn't her at all. This isn't my house, there is no second
chance, nothing, no one, is coming back. Where's my
baseball glove? I ask her, and she answers sweetly, like she
always does, If it was up your ass you'd know where it was.
ACTION. We are in the kitchen, holding our breath, I am
writing these notes, I am in prison, I am making a movie
of being in prison, the brain can contain anything, in its
little hall of mirrors. We watch the way Julianne's mouth
forms the words, *I tried so hard,* though there really is only
one way to say *snake,* to say *flower,* to say *gun.* But we
need someone to say it to us first, to point into the cage,
to point to the sky, to say the word.

  CUT.

I finally get to change out of these wet jeans, Julianne
whispers, as she passes by me. Without thinking I reach
out and hug her.

from *the reenactments*

kahn & selesnick, *faerie*
(maeve dances with bat), 2015

Are you sure—one would like to ask—that it cannot love you back?

ON COMPULSION

I keep returning to the burning house. I think
Freud would call it the compulsion to return to the
scene of early trauma. I think he'd think I was
trying to gain some mastery over that situation,
mastery that I lacked as a child, but who knows
if this is true, or if I will. It's strange. You suggested
that "I could do this in private," that I could just
write my poems in my room, put them on a shelf.
I did that for a long time, that's what writers do.
No one's going to see or should see 99.9% of what
we write. You know, one sect of Buddhism has
this practice where you write three memoirs. One
of them is public, one of them is private, and
one of them is secret. The secret one is usually the
biggest, the most massive. A lot of it isn't what
you're ashamed of necessarily—what we publish,
ideally, is just what belongs in the world, what
might help the world in some way, by putting it out
there. A lot of the stuff I write would in no way
help the world. It wouldn't help anyone.

patricia weaver francisco & christopher vondracek
talk with nick flynn, hamline university, 2016

Nebuchadnezzar
(The Father)

Three girls in the park begin to
sing something holy, a song with a
lost room inside it

as their prayerbook comes unglued

& scatters.

from *some ether*

ON MADNESS

I once heard that the voice of madness
is compelling because it uses your own
voice to convince you to, say, wander
into traffic, or climb a tower with a
rifle. If the voice was unfamiliar you
might not believe it so readily. If the
voice was unfamiliar it might get you
to see that there are other ways of
being, other options. It might allow
you to see a way to break out of the
patterns you are trapped by, patterns
you no longer even see.

Traffic, towers, rifles . . . the
world is vast and filled with voices. If
you live in New York, then the voices
that rise up from that island of power
and creativity can seem the only ones
worth listening to—you know it's
wrong but you also don't really believe
it's wrong. They sing to you all night.
This might be true with anywhere,
if you only listen to the voices of those
who live next door, who look like you.

from the foreword to *guernica: annual*, 2014

josh neufeld, *father outside*, 2004

nick flynn, *aka joe russo*, 1988

JOE RUSSO

No one knows how long Joe Russo has been skulking
around Pine Street. Ten years? Twenty? He'd pass through
the doors like another man's shadow, his face pressed to
the wall, almost part of the wall, like he's using it to pull
himself along. Mumbling and squirrelly, small with large
hands, a hooked nose, his graying hair slicked back. Joe
Russo never sleeps in a bed, never lines up with the rest,
almost no one has spoken to him in all these years.
    Some mornings, when I punch out, he's lurking
around the cars. Some days I ask if he wants to get some
breakfast. One day, to my surprise, he says yes. We walk
over a bridge to a diner in Southie, where he nearly gets
us killed by muttering about the "hippies" in the adjacent
booth, whom I would describe as "bikers." We begin
having breakfast once a week. As I get to know him I ask
the basics—family, Social Security number, last residence,

work history—all spotty. The psych people have nothing on him, though he says he took "nerve pills" at one point, and that they helped.

One morning he asks me why I call him Joe, that his name is Matthew. Matthew Maltese. I have no idea where the name Joe Russo came from and it turns out neither does he. He tells me that when he walks along the streets he can hear his father's voice calling him, *Matthew, Matthew, Matthew*, that he's always moving either away or toward that voice. Now that I know his real name I take him to the Social Security Administration offices to see if they have him in their computers. It turns out he's been getting a disability check for the past twenty years, and that this check's been going to his brother, a middle-class guy living in a nice suburb, who's Matthew's payee. In the beginning the brother would drive into Boston, find Matthew, buy him a meal, some new clothes, leave him with fifty out of a three-hundred-dollar check. Sometimes even take him home for a few days, wash him up. But after a while the brother came into the city less and less. The checks kept coming, the brother ended up putting an addition on his house, a sunroom off the kitchen. When they sat across from each other in the Brown Lobby, after twelve years without a word, Matthew deadpanned, *I haven't seen you around lately, where've you been?*

from *another bullshit night in suck city*

THE PISS OF GOD

Sometimes a man falls asleep in the midst of
buttoning his jacket, his fingers hanging on to the
last button. Sometimes, embedded in hot asphalt,
you see a key, shined by the soles of pedestrians'
shoes. You check your pockets, suddenly worried.
The sidewalk calls, using the trick of gravity to
bring you to your knees, to close your eyes, to make
you sleep. If there's grass, if you can see it, each
blade catches a sliver of streetlight, each blade wants
you to hold on. Face down you swear you can feel
the earth spin, hold tight or you'll spin off into
outer space. Forget about ceilings, about walls, about
doors, about keys. The bread you ate at lunch is
already turning to soil inside you, nightsoil now,
darkness hovering inside. Soon your flesh will
crumble off you, those on their way to work the
next morning will pass your whitened skeleton like
so many styrofoam cups—bleached, perfect.
    If not for the rats you could crawl beneath a
bush. A bush. A bench. A bridge. The alliterative
universe. Rats too can pass through that needle's
eye to enter heaven, as easily as they pass into a box
imagined into a house. Houses inside buildings,
houses inside tunnels, some exist for only a
day, some, miraculously, longer. This box held a
refrigerator, the refrigerator is in an apartment,
a man is in the box. Tomorrow the box will be
flattened and tossed, you've seen the garbage men
stomping them down to fit into the truck. Wake up
on the grass, soaking wet. Dew is the piss of God.
Another bullshit night in suck city, my father mutters.
    And then there's the Celtics, losing just across
town. Last night Mackie had a la-z-boy set up in
Rat Alley, watching a television hotwired into a light
pole. I stepped into Mackie's living room, checked
out a couple minutes of play—can these still be
called the glory days of Bird? Step out of your room,
settle into a discarded recliner—are you inside now
or out? Position your chair before your television,
take your walk, find your coffee, by morning it all
will be gone—no inside no outside, no cardboard
box no mansion, no birth no death, no container no

contained, a Zen koan, a frikkin riddle. A garbage truck hauled the tv away, another will be put out on the sidewalk tonight. But a la-z-boy, my lord, maybe not again in this lifetime.

from *another bullshit night in suck city*

nick flynn, *grate* (robert de niro on set of *being flynn*), 2011

WINTER

(1989) My father wraps himself in
newspaper some nights, stuffs his coat
with newspaper, the headlines finally
about him, though he isn't named.
Just more heartstring pieces about "the
homeless." *Get it straight, I've never
flung a knife or shot a bullet at anyone.
I've only been locked up for two of my fifty-
nine years. I'm no jailbird.* The nights
drop below freezing and still he sleeps
outside. "My toes," he writes me, "are
being cut off." On wet nights he wraps
himself in plastic, a Hefty trashbag
sealed with duct tape, he weaves
himself a cocoon, lies on the ground,
puts his feet into the bag and pushes
until they reach the bottom. Leaning
forward, he tightens the plastic around
his ankles and tapes them, and then
he tapes the bag around his waist.
This way, in the night, the bag won't
slide down his body.

from *another bullshit night in suck city*

JONATHAN ROBINSON FLYNN
President

THE FACT FOUNDATION of AMERICA
INCORPORATED

104 CHARLES STREET, #102 BEACON HILL
BOSTON, MASSACHUSETTS 02114
617/227-0080

December 21, 1986

Dear Nicholas,

Merry Christmas! I am a born
writer. So are you! Several evenings ago
on T.V. a cry went out, "We — America,
needs another John Steinbeck!" — I am
the man! — The poor, the homeless,
the sad people in America need
a strong voice. I do hope that
what I can't say — you will.

My deep love always,

your Father, Jonathan

a letter from my father (written a month
before he became homeless), 1986

ULYSSES

Many fathers are gone. Some leave, some are left.
Some return, unknown and hungry. Only the dog
remembers. Even if around, most disappear all
day, to jobs their children only slightly understand.
Gone to office, gone to shop, men in suits hiding
behind closed doors, yelling into phones, men in
coveralls, reading pornography in pickup trucks.
The carpenter. The electrician. They drive to
strangers' houses, a woman in a robe answers the
door, they sit at the table with her, she offers coffee
and cake, they talk about the day ahead. *By nightfall
you won't recognize the bathroom*, he promises. *Monday
we start in on the roof.* Many end up sitting around
the house all day, sneaking sips in the woodshed.
Many drive to other towns, make love to a woman
they've been making love to for years. Some continue
to yell at their sons from the grave, some are less
than a tattered photograph. Some sons need to
exhume the body, some need to see a name written
in a ledger. Some drive past a house the father once
lived in as a child, park across from it, some swear
that if they could gaze into his face just once their
hearts would settle. One friend inherited some
money and hired a private investigator to track down
his lost father, paid a thousand dollars to find out
his father was dead. All my life my father had been
manifest as an absence, a non-presence, a name
without a body. The three of us sat around the
table, my mother, brother and I, all carrying his
name. *Flynn?*

Some part of me knew he would show up, that if
I stood in one place long enough he would find me,
like you're taught to do when you're lost. But they
never taught us what to do if both of you are lost,
and you both end up in the same place, waiting.

from *another bullshit night in suck city*

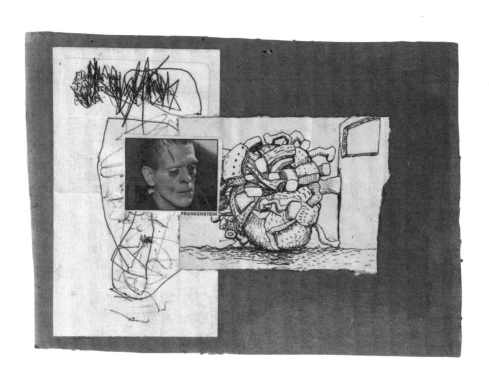

nick flynn, *friend*, 2011

HAM

Noah had grandiose plans to save the world. Noah, it
should be remembered, was a disreputable man who heard
a voice. The villagers, his neighbors, laughed. Noah, a
bit of a drunk, was not taken seriously. The voice said, *By
what you make you will save the world.* And so, reluctantly
at first, Noah began his life's work, an impossible project,
something much larger than himself. But at night Noah
was again filled with doubt, and he drank to quiet the
voices. The people in his village spoke behind their hands
as he passed, touched their caps, smiled. The village
was miles from the ocean and Noah was spending his days
building a boat—*Made it out of hic-kory barky-barky.*
Noah had three sons—Shem, Ham, and Japheth.
Ham came upon his father one day, naked and ranting,
building his impossible boat in a blackout. God had
spoken, God kept speaking, God wouldn't stop speaking.
For witnessing his father naked and drunk, Ham and all
his offspring became accursed forever, to the end of time.

My father may not hear voices, but he also has an impossible
project, he's also filled with a force larger than himself.
In nearly every letter my father has sent me for the last
twenty-five years he tells me his writing is going very, very
well. His novel, such as it is, if it is at all, written in blackout
and prison, is his ark, the thing that will save him,
that will save the world. His single-mindedness impresses
most, his fathomless belief in his own greatness, in his
powers to transform a failed world, to make it whole again
by a word, by a story. That if you stick with your vision
long enough you will be redeemed. All this in the face
of near-constant evidence to the contrary. The actual
circumstances of his life—his alcoholism, the crimes he's
committed, his homelessness and decades of poverty—
these are mere tests, and what is a faith not tested? Noah
needed to gather nails, to sort the animals, to convince
his sons. He planed his timber and laid out the ribs. His ark
would be bigger than the temple. We all need to create
the story that will make sense of our lives, to make sense
of the daily tasks. Yet each night the doubts returned,
howling through him. Without doubt there can be no faith.
At daybreak Noah looked to the darkening sky and vowed
to work faster. My father cannot die, he tells me, will not,

until his work is completed. But is there a deadline inside
him for when he must finish, a day like Noah, when the
rains begin? When the boat, finished or not, begins to rise
from the cradle?

Within a week after seeing him wrapped in a bedsheet and
ranting, his bare feet in a pool of his own piss, my father
has gone down even further, each night coming into the
shelter drunker, more abusive, more out of control.
He takes a swing at Cookie, calls her a "dyke cunt," but
Cookie gives him another chance, merely puts him out for
the night—*He's your father, for chrissakes.* But by the end of
the week, when I arrive at nine for my shift, my co-workers
look at me wearily—they've had another long night
battling him. I've chosen to leave it to them, to escape the
building, to spend my nights driving the streets. Finally,
he is brought up for barring:

> 13 Feb 89
> Jon was OFN this evening, and when he was told he
> had to go to the Laundry Room he exploded into
> anger. He started yelling and screaming racial slurs,
> lesbian cracks, verbal threats and every swear he
> could think of toward Dianne and Cookie. He was
> highly intoxicated, very upset and unmanageable.
> He was finally escorted by Paul and he was shouting
> and swearing all the way down the alley. Jon has
> created problems in housing and this is not his first
> outburst at the front door. When he is intoxicated
> he is extremely hard to handle and it's time for BH20
> and a rest for the staff.

Stamped in for "BH20 or Bar," meaning if he refuses to
go to the thirty-day lockup detox at Bridgewater State
Correctional Facility he will be barred for at least two
months. He's described as "w/m, 5'7", white hair, slanted
eye, gray stubble, 150 lbs." I know my father will never
voluntarily check himself back into prison. At the change-
of-shift meetings his barring is voted on. I am at one of
these meetings. The vote goes nine bar, one against,
and one abstention. I would like to say that I abstained
from the voting, but I don't remember if this is true.
It is just as likely that I voted to bar my father, in support
of my co-workers.

The rains, as we all know, did come. The boat lifted above the drowned world, and the disbelievers perished, and no one was more surprised than Noah. The first right thing he'd done, and it came from obeying a voice only he could hear, which others took as proof of his madness. But what of Ham? It didn't matter if he told anyone about his drunken father or not, if he chided him or tried to dress him, if he lifted his struggling body back into bed, if he took his hand and told him where to place his feet, none of this changed the fact of what he'd seen. It's possible he opened a door innocently, followed the sound of Noah's voice cursing God and the sky, possible he didn't even look, that he turned away before seeing. And it's likely that Noah hadn't noticed the door opening, couldn't have told you who had come in, which son, wouldn't remember anyway. Apparently, it's God's call. Ham saw his father drunken and naked, and for this he was cursed, and all of his offspring, and the races that led from these offspring, accursed forever.

from *another bullshit night in suck city*

Proteus is at the bottom of a steep cliff, down a treacherous path, at the edge of the sea. From the top of the cliff you can see him, sitting on a flat rock, staring into the endless nothing of the sea, but to reach him is difficult. You've been told that he has the answer to your question, and you are a little desperate to have this question answered. As you make your way down you must be careful not to dislodge any loose gravel, careful not to cry out when the thorns pierce your feet. You must approach him as quietly as you can, get right up on him, get your hands on him, around his neck. You've been told that you have to hold on while you ask your question, you've been told that you can't let go. You've been told that as you hold on Proteus will transform into the shape and form of that which most terrifies you, in order to get you to release your grip. But the promise is that if you can hold on, through your terror, he will return to his true form and answer your question.

I get to the edge of knowing, then teeter back and forth—it's what makes these visits shimmer. It is all we can do, all I've ever done—stand before what I know, and pulse into the unknown.

from *the reenactments*

AFTERMATH
(ONE YEAR LATER)

*questions often asked &
some possible answers*

Q: Was writing the book cathartic
for you?
    A: In my experience,
whatever happens clings
to us like barnacles on the
hull of a ship, slowing us
slightly, both uglifying and
giving us texture. You can
scrape all you want, you
can, if you have money, hire
someone else to scrape,
but the barnacles will come
back, or at least leave
a blemish on the steel.

Q: Why didn't you label your father
mentally ill?
    A: Another reader, whose
father apparently was
manic-depressive, criticized
me for this, though my
father was never diagnosed
thus. It would be easier, I
sometimes think, if I *could*
label him mentally ill, and
point to that and say that's
why he was homeless, and
we could all sleep easier,
knowing he was not like us.

Q: How do you deal with making
people sad with what you write?
    A: I'm beginning to
believe that nearly all
questions are projections
of some inner need on the
questioner's part, as if
he had a movie projector

inside his head, showing
the same movie over and
over. I thought I was the
only one who did this, and
it's comforting to know
I'm not alone.

Q: Do you feel you shot yourself in the
foot with the title?
    A:

Q: What did you feel the first time you
saw your father homeless?
    A: Not to be coy, but there
was no moment I could nail
down for you—it was more a
series of steps, a progression,
one moment flowing into
the next, which I believe is
the experience, for most, of
finding oneself in a difficult
situation—you cannot
believe it is really happening,
that all roads have led to
this, and that you may be
stuck there for an undefined
number of days or even
years. And so, for me, there
was also no single emotion,
even if I could find a moment
to attach it to—one
emotion transformed into
another, often in a more
associative rather than a
logical way—confusion into
giddiness, outrage into an
inappropriate joy, numbness
into hyperawareness—
which is the way life has
been for me, so far at least,
though I expect not
even that will remain fixed.

Q: Your father identifies himself as a storyteller. What is the purpose of telling stories?

A: If one were a Buddhist, one might say we spend much of our lives in "monkey-mind," swinging from story to story, our thoughts never quiet. Perhaps it is our fear, that in the silence between stories, in the moment of falling, the fear that we will never find the one story which will save us, and so we lunge for another, and we feel safe again, if only for as long as we are telling it.

Q: You've said elsewhere that you based the structure of the book on *Moby-Dick*, comparing Ahab's obsessive search with your own circling of your father. Can you say more about this?

A: In *Moby-Dick*, the eponymous whale doesn't appear until the last fifty pages. The story of the whale appears earlier, but the actual whale only breaks the surface for a moment at the end, just long enough to wreak havoc and pull Ahab under. The whole book is about a whale and the whale isn't there. In the end the central mystery remains unfathomable—what was it exactly that Ahab gave his life to? We know he lost his leg, and that that loss became a story, and the story became the obsession that in the end defined, and ended, his life. We have to be careful of the stories we tell about ourselves.

Q: Do you give money to panhandlers?

A: Sometimes, even though I know I'm not supposed to. Sometimes I don't give, even though I can feel the quarters in my pocket, and the person looks really hungry or in bad shape. Then I don't feel good for a while, or else I forget about it immediately. Sometimes I give only to someone who looks ill, sometimes only to someone who looks healthy. I am completely confused and overwhelmed by the whole transaction.

Q: Has your father read the book? How does he feel about it?

A: I've answered that question in many ways, and each answer I gave seemed true when I said it, but now I marvel at my certainty. I said that since the book came out it seemed that he was, to my surprise, more lucid, more compassionate, and that he seemed, when I saw him, not to be as drunk as other times I'd seen him (placing me, by comparison, once again firmly in the "normal" end of the spectrum). I might have even said, with a straight

face and more than once,
that perhaps the book had
given some meaning to his
life (ah, the transformative
powers of art!), a reason
not to drift so far out, to
hold it together (aka *my Jesus
complex*). After having seen
him again ten months after
the book came out, raging
and incoherent, I realize it
was all a self-aggrandizing
delusion, though perhaps it
was simply the wrong time
of the month.

Q: Do you think your father had talent?
    A: Several people have
gotten in touch with me
since the book came out,
people who knew my
father years before I did,
and some have testified to
how much they admired
his drive and talent as a
writer. My father's not
dead yet, so there's always
still the chance the Nobel
committee will call.

Q: Do you still blame yourself for your
mother's suicide?
    A: Do you really think I'm
going to answer that here?

    addendum to the paperback edition
    of *another bullshit night in suck city*

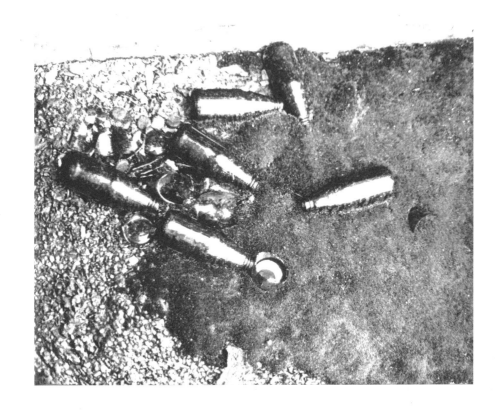

nick flynn, *boston*, 1988

STRAW TO A DROWNING MAN

ACT 1, SCENE 2
Lights up. Morning. Television off. Gideon is squeezed in beside Alice on the chair, asleep with his head on her shoulder. His suit collar turned up, his hair disheveled. Alice is reading a book. As Alice reads Gideon slowly wakes up, realizes he's been leaning on her. Embarrassed, he straightens himself, but remains sitting beside her. A box of donuts is balanced on the arm of the chair beside Alice—she takes one. She comes upon a passage in the book, eats donut as she speaks.

Alice   (*musing*) Straw to a drowning man. *Straw* to a drowning man. A drowning man. A man drowning. (*beat*) I've never been able to wrap my mind around that one—you see a man drowning, you throw him a straw. (*beat*) What exactly does the drowning man do with the straw? I mean, does he use it like a snorkel, to breathe underwater? Does he simply hold on to it, like a tiny life raft—hey, drowning guy, grab on to this, a thousand more and you got yourself a boat. (*musing*) Does he use it to drink the ocean or puddle or whatever it is he's drowning in, thus hurrying his demise, ending his misery? Is it the same straw that broke the camel's back, the proverbial "last straw," that last little bit which somehow pulls him under? (*looks at Gideon*) What kind of straw are we talking about here?

Gideon looks at Alice, he stands, looks around, still groggy. Phone rings. Gideon looks around for source of sound. Alice pulls cellphone from chair cushions, opens it.

Alice   Who? He's not here. What? Your phone? How do I know that? (*closes phone, then speaks to audience*) Straw. I mean, you're close enough to hand him a straw, or a piece of straw, why don't you take his hand and pull him out?

Gideon   That phone works?

Alice   I told you. (*takes another donut from the box, offers it in an offhand way*) You hungry?

Gideon   No. Could I . . . ?

ACT 3, SCENE 4
Lights up. Ivan is standing beside wheelbarrow, bleary, rope still tied to his waist. Gideon is in Alice's chair. Gideon pushing his feet into a large trashbag and pulling it up the length of his body, duct-taping it around his ankles, his waist, his chest. Beside him, a camp stove is heating a pan of water, donuts stacked in a few small towers beside it. The television flickers on—Alice's head appears on-screen. Gideon glances at television while Alice speaks, but tries to ignore her. At first Ivan apparently doesn't hear or notice Alice.

Alice   (*staring straight ahead*) Grasping at straws. (*beat*) When do you ever actually get to see a man drowning? Maybe once in your life, maybe twice, if you're lucky. At that moment you either save him or you don't. You either try or you don't . . .

Ivan turns toward sound of television, moves toward it, accidentally kicks over a tower of donuts.

Gideon   (*annoyed*) Careful.

Ivan   (*confused*) They changed the channel.

Alice   . . . and then you go on, you live with it, your choice. Maybe you froze when you could have jumped, maybe from that moment on you tell yourself that nothing could have been done. Maybe that's what you have to tell yourself, maybe it's true. Maybe your name was in the paper as a hero, maybe as an onlooker, maybe the person drowning was you.

from *alice invents a little game &*
alice always wins

Alice: Straw to a Drowning Man

guy barash, *alice invents a little game
& alice always wins* (opera), 2016

WHO DIED & MADE YOU KING?

(1974) If, without taking your eyes from the television,
you call out for a glass of water and your mother,
stirring some onions in a pan, answers, Who died
and made you king?—it might make you wonder
if you were, in fact, a king. Unknown, unrecognized,
but still—a king. Or, if you call out for a glass of
water and your mother, as she passes on her way out
to work, answers, Who was your slave yesterday?—
it might mean something else. Or it might mean
the same thing, for kings, after all, often have slaves,
the two often go together, you know this.
  In school you study the Civil Rights
Movement, but you aren't interested in civil rights.
You're interested in the Middle Ages, a time of kings
and dungeons, which they don't teach in school.
Medieval, you like to say the word, it has the word
"evil" in it. Today the teacher is talking about
Martin Luther King—every year you learn the
same four things about Martin Luther King—but
you are thinking about Nebuchadnezzar, the king
of ancient Babylon. God took away his kingdom in
order to punish him for his pride, and then God
condemned him to live in the woods like an animal.
God, apparently, doesn't like one to have pride.
For seven years Nebuchadnezzar lived without

society or the ability to think. Hair grew all over his body, his nails became claws.

You look at your own hand, stretch your fingers out.

Martin Luther King sat in a Birmingham jail, locked up for supporting the right for a man to order a sandwich whenever and wherever he damn well pleased. Your father is in prison, your mother told you so, the prison is in Missouri, but that's all you've heard. From the big map on the wall, the one you stare at when you're supposed to be listening, you know Missouri is in the middle of nowhere. The teacher says that while in prison Martin Luther King wrote a letter. You were supposed to read the letter for homework. *Can anyone tell us one thing he wrote in his letter?* She looks straight at you as she says this—you blur your eyes and she dissolves.

Back home, belly-down on the floor, you read the funnies while your mother reads the obituaries. You look for *The Wizard of Id*—you like Spook, the troll-like guy, chained up forever in that dungeon. You like how every time Spook appears he tries to escape, and you both want him to make it and want him to be there the next time you visit.

One day your mother passes on a letter your father has sent you from prison. In the envelope, along with the one-page letter, he has included a clipping from the newspaper—*The Wizard of Id*. Spook is chained to a wall, a hooded man holding a whip stands behind him.

If you ask your mother why your father is in prison she might say, *Your father is a reprobate.* Since you don't know what a reprobate is, you might think it's a type of king.

But it's more likely that you'll think it's a type of spook.

Your father, from what you remember, from the one time you remember meeting him, looks like a cross between Andy Williams and the Cowardly Lion. All of your mother's boyfriends remind you of someone you've seen on tv. Tom Jones. Dick Cavett. Gregg Allman.

One day you will learn that what was once Babylon is now Iraq. Years later, after your country

invades, its king, its president, will be found, some
months later, hiding in what will be called a "spider
hole"—his beard gone wild, his nails grown long.
And some days after this, after he is sentenced to
death, he will be hung by the neck by jeering hooded
men. You will watch his execution on the same
day you see a photograph of a lost pop star showing
her pussy to the world.

But for now it is still that beautiful spring day,
and you are still inside. Your mother hasn't gone
out yet. Tonight she'll tend bar until two, but she
doesn't have to go in until dark—anything could
still happen. The two of you could head down to
the harbor, get some ice cream, park by Peggotty
Beach, watch the summer people try to swim in the
still-cold Atlantic. You could help her chop carrots
and onions for her chicken stew. You could drive
around the cliffs, past all the big houses teetering
on the edge of the ocean, make bets on which will
be pulled in next. But if she's going out to meet her
latest boyfriend, the cop (Elvis), it wouldn't make
sense for you to go with her. What would you do,
play with his gun again while they make out in the
front seat? As she passes you on her way out, you
are still belly-down, now staring into your box of
shadows—*The Three Stooges* now, Curly's head in
a vice again, Moe cutting into it with a hacksaw.
Moe, it seems, is forever trying to carve his way into
someone else's body.

from *The Ticking Is the Bomb*

ONE SIMPLE QUESTION

(1995) I'm working as an itinerant
poet in New York City Public
Schools—Harlem, the South Bronx,
Crown Heights—reading poems to
young people, helping them to write
their own. These are the years of
unprecedented wealth in the United
States, and if you want to find the
worst public school in any city you just
have to look up the one named after
Martin Luther King. The schools I
work in are in neighborhoods that look
like Dresden after the firebombing,
though the carpetbaggers, the
speculators, are already making
inroads, buying up the burned-out
shells. To start a class I sometimes
read the poem "A Story That Could
Be True" by William Stafford. It deals,
in part, with a missing father, and I
know that the fathers of many of these
kids are missing. The poem starts:

> If you were exchanged in the
> cradle and your real mother died
> without ever telling the story
> then no one knows your name,
> and somewhere in the world
> your father is lost and needs you
> but you are far away.

I'd choke up every time I'd read it out
loud, for reasons that were mysterious
to me then but seem obvious now.
For six years my father had lived like
Nebuchadnezzar, without society or
the ability to think—hair grew all over
his body, his nails became claws.

He can never find
how true you are, how ready.
When the great wind comes
and the robberies of the rain
you stand on the corner shivering.
The people who go by—
you wonder at their calm.

By the time I was reading Stafford to
second-graders in Harlem, my father
had been off the streets for nearly
five years, living in his government-
subsidized studio apartment in
downtown Boston. But once again
I'd lost contact with him, once again
he'd slipped into the shadows. Or I
had. When I found him again I told
myself I wanted to ask him just one
simple question—how had he met
my mother?—but I had to keep going
back, for it took years for him to
answer this question.

from *The Ticking Is the Bomb*

ON TIME

Q: What do you think are the primary forces that come to bear on your perception of past events?

A: Time is certainly one of the primary forces, this wonderful and terrifying ether we are carried along by, briefly. When I started *Another Bullshit Night in Suck City*, I think I had some biblical fervor that I could actually embody my mother through language, that if I got it right she would rise from the page—the word made flesh. Or that I could somehow understand the deep mystery of my father through words, yet he is still an utter enigma to me (as I write those words I wonder if it is still true, or if time has actually given me some insights into my father, if only for the fact that I am approaching the age he was when he ended up on the streets . . .). In the following memoir, *The Ticking Is the Bomb*, I was wrestling with becoming a father myself, and found that the central mysteries of fatherhood only deepened—what could I learn from my own father beyond what not to do? Yet without him I wouldn't exist. It is a more interior book, which means it is less determined (what kind of father will I be?), where *Another Bullshit Night in Suck City* is a journey, where the outcome is already known at the outset (the father will make it off the streets alive). In the third book, *The Reenactments*, the mother and father are now played by actors, for a film, so the hope of them rising from the page, embodied, is replaced with light. They are now projections on a screen, which is perhaps closer to our experience of memory, which is all I've ever been working with.

susan landry talks with nick flynn,
run to the roundhouse, nellie, 2014

nick flynn, *father murderer* (robert de niro
on set of *being flynn*), 2011

FATHER MURDERER

(2011) January, record snowfall, snow everywhere, more
coming. Six weeks before shooting is to begin I get a
call from Paul that De Niro wants to meet my father. He
wants to go to the shelter. He wants to go the next day.
It's Sunday, De Niro is in New York, I'm in Texas, due to
teach the next day, my first day of classes. We can take the
train up to Boston, Paul tells me, use the time to talk
about the movie, about my father. He means the train from
New York. I hang up and go online and book a flight. I'm
on a plane in three hours. I cancel my classes.

In New York the next morning it's snowing—
sleeting, really. The radio says that the trains are delayed,
that the airports will close. I get a message to meet at
Paul's hotel at nine, plans have changed—we are not taking
the train, we will meet De Niro at an airport in New
Jersey, a private airport, where a private jet will fly us to
Boston. Two pilots are waiting for us, the rain has turned
to snow. This is the way it is, nothing will stop us from
this trip. Inside the plane it is like a yacht—leather couches,
reclining chairs, enough seats for maybe six people. It's
not costing us a thing, I'm told—De Niro has credit here,
he's owed a flight. I warn them that my father is much
diminished, that he is not the same man as the man
De Niro will be portraying—the menace is gone, he's
grown old, lost his fight, toothless now.

On the plane I sit across the aisle from De Niro, lean in
to him as he speaks, but the engine is beside our heads
and he speaks softly, so it is hard to make out the words—
something about his kids, how one needs to be moved
to a school closer to his home, how he is starting to have
some trouble. The boy's mother, who is not with De Niro
now, I assume, maybe she's in California, but I can only
understand half of what he is saying. I keep flashing to
his hand, wrapped in that white towel, how it pops into
flame after he shoots Fanucci in the face, how he watches
Fanucci fall, how only then does he notice his hand
burning, how he shakes it, his eyes still on the fallen
body, how the towel unwraps, how he puts the fire out.
De Niro is talking to me, but I am having a hard time
hearing the words. It seems as if even he is having trouble
finding the right place, the right school, for his kids.

It is impossible to know what shape we will find my father in. I worry he will be lost, incoherent. Yet when we show up at Roscommon he's awake, in the lunchroom (maybe they call it a dayroom?), and lucid. The television is on, each seat taken (The Next Holiday is EASTER). It is a grim place, though the shelter will be grimmer. My father's apartment, by the time I moved him out, was grimmer. Here he has three meals a day, he has nurses and orderlies, he is taken care of, which is perhaps all he ever desired, aside from fame. And now I am introducing him to Robert De Niro, who will play him in the film version of his life. We move to an empty room. I usually bring a copy of the memoir with me, as it seems to jog his memory (to hold it in his hands, to scan the pages that talk about his childhood, his nights in the shelter, his time in prison), but I realize I forgot to bring it. I know him so well, after writing the book, and yet I barely know him at all. I get to the edge of knowing, then teeter back and forth—that's what makes these visits shimmer. It is all we can do, all I've ever done—stand before what I know, and pulse into the unknown. For years I could not imagine what my father would be like outside of alcohol, yet here he is—he hasn't had a drink since he's been inside Roscommon. His stories are different now, not as scripted, yet in many ways the damage is done. My father is eighty—from the life he's led it's a miracle he's alive. I'd have died a hundred deaths by now, if I'd continued to drink like he drank. I forgot to bring my book, but it turns out De Niro has a copy. He pulls it out of his bag—dog-eared, heavily underlined, notes written in the margins. This is Robert De Niro, I tell my father. The actor who will play you in the film we are making about your life. My father nods, doesn't seem impressed. And this is Paul, the director—he also wrote the script. Very nice to meet you both, my father says, though he has, over the years, met Paul a few times before. I show him the book, remind him that it's about him, about his life. I point to my name on the cover—he is, as always, impressed. A book? How'd you figure that out? What promoted you? I point to the title, remind him that it's something he said, that he always was good with titles, which allows him to begin, to start talking about himself. It's like turning the handle on a jack-in-the-box, and out come his stories. Amazing that the stories are still inside him, that he can still find them.

He holds forth for an hour, one tangent leads to another. When I try to bring him around to the film we're making he cuts me off: Let me speak, you wonton fucken goonball. We all smile. Paul writes *wonton fucken goonball* in his notebook. I take this moment to try, once again, to get him to take it in, that we are making a film about his life. Bob is going to play you, in the movie version of this book. That's why we're here, he wanted to meet you. He looks over at De Niro, as if taking him in for the first time. So, you do a little acting? my father asks. You like to act? De Niro smiles, shrugs: Yeah, I do a little acting.

My father is not surprised, nor seemingly impressed, that a movie is being made of his life. He has always assumed one would be, since he is the most interesting person he's ever met (*only two people can play me—either Dustin Hoffman or myself*). After asking De Niro if he liked to act, after De Niro shrugs, I tell my father, He was in *The Godfather*. *The Godfather*? my father echoes. *That's a big deal*. He narrows his eyes, takes De Niro in more fully. He *is* the godfather, I say.

Sometimes, in a movie theater, waiting for the movie to begin, the lights start to dim, gradually, and for a moment you're unsure if the room is going dark or if it's your eyes, failing. Sometimes you find yourself in a public restroom— often in an airport, on your way somewhere (where?)— standing before the automatic faucet, waving your hands, but the water does not come, the sensor doesn't sense you. Sometimes, when you try to move your cursor, the trackpad doesn't register your fingertip, the cursor doesn't move. You are both frozen—for those few moments it is as if you do not exist.

Before we leave Roscommon, I take pictures of my father with De Niro, of Paul with my father, of Paul and De Niro with my father. The only camera we have is on my phone. I pass it to Paul and he takes a few pictures of me and De Niro with my father, but later I discover that none of the shots with me in them come out. Later, when I show these pictures to people, I have to explain that I was there, that that is my father, that Paul took the pictures, but something happened.

An hour later, at Pine Street, no one recognizes De Niro—his hat pulled down low, he keeps covering his face with a handkerchief, as if he had a cold. I point out what I remember—the cage, the front desk, the showers, the dorm. De Niro notices that no one is walking as if beaten down, as if ashamed. Maybe this is their home, I say, or maybe if they look vulnerable they become marks. We stay for an hour or so, see what we have to see, then we go. On the plane home De Niro says that in the film he needs to be able to ramble on, to hold forth, like my father had just done with him. Two days later I hand over six pages of monologues, demented psycho ramblings, distilled versions of things my father has said to me over the years. Rants like this, when he's being thrown out of the shelter, words that will likely rattle around inside me forever:

Where is he? FATHER MURDERER. Come out and face me. What does he know? He knows shit. He's killing himself in this cesspool, he can't even see it. Where is he hiding, in some little closet, sucking mama's tit? FATHER MURDERER. Come out and face me, coward. I could have jerked off and flushed you down the toilet. FATHER MURDERER. Face me.

from *the reenactments*

FOUR (MORE) MONOLOGUES

[pp 62–63 scene 113]

I'm only twenty-eight years old, why do I look
like this? What happened to my body? I've dug
ditches, worked as a longshoreman. In Florida I
was Barracuda Buck, Native Guide—no one else
would put their hands in the barracuda's mouth.
I sold encyclopedias door to door—*Encyclopedia
Britannica*—broads'd come to the door in their
nightgowns, I'd say, Excuse me, Madam, is your
husband home? Hell no, come on in . . . I'm only
twenty-eight years old, what happened to my body?
Why do I look like this? What are you looking at?

[p66 top scene 115]

You are me. I created you. Your dear mother, if she
were here today, I know she would be with me, I
have no doubt, no doubt at all. She was beautiful,
for chrissakes. If she were here she'd say the same
thing—you are me.

[p69 scene 128]

In the beginning was the word—Salinger, Twain,
Jonathan Robinson Flynn. I was put on this earth
to help other people, I was put on this earth to write
my masterpiece. And it is written. My masterpiece
will save the world. By a word I will save the
world. The confessions of Christopher Cobb! I am
Christopher Cobb! Everything I've seen, everything
I've done, every experience, is there, in the book,
it is all there, everything, in the book! It is all there,
the entire world. In a word. Each word is a world.
Hundreds of them. Thousands. Let me speak, you
wonton fucken goonball. I am a poet. Let me speak!

[p70 scene 130]

Pederasts. Priests. Without faith you are nothing.
The words don't line up. I stood behind the priest,
I held his robe as he put the host on each tongue.
All the girls, lined up, their tongues out, the disc
dissolving. Impotente sanctitus domine domino
suck my cock-o. Faith. Without faith you are lost.
Without faith you are nothing. You. Are. Nothing.

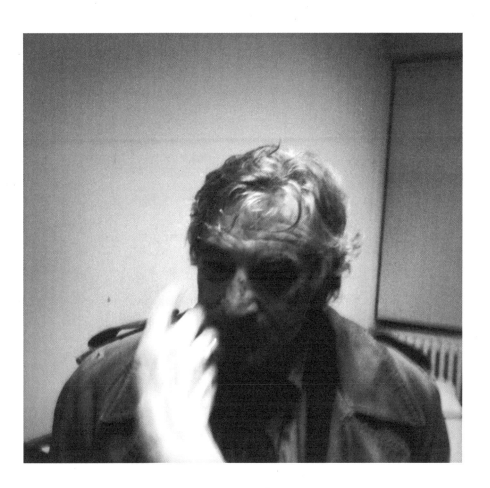

nick flynn, *beaten* (robert de niro on
set of *being flynn*), 2011

THE INVENTOR OF THE LIFE RAFT

His father, my father claims, invented both the life raft and
the power window, though sometimes it is the life raft
and the push-button lock on car doors. Or some sort of
four-gig carburetor that saves gas. In this story my father's
family is rich, with gardeners and chauffeurs during the
Depression. His grandfather owned a roofing company
that had contracts for Faneuil Hall and the Boston
Museum of Fine Arts—big public works projects that kept
them flush while the country struggled. Look inside the
grasshopper weathervane on the roof of Faneuil Hall and
you will see my great-grandfather's name—Thaddeus—
which is also my brother's name. My father tells me this,
but how to get inside this grasshopper he doesn't say.

After months of calling the U.S. Patent Office in Washington,
of asking where I might locate the original patent for the
invention of the life raft, I am directed to the Science,
Industry, and Business Library on Madison Avenue, just
across the river. There I waste a few more days online
before someone finally takes pity on me and directs me to
the back room, which houses the actual books of all the
patents issued for every year, starting before the Civil War.
As I don't know the date of the supposed invention, I must
look in each volume, under the last name Flynn, from 1900
on up. I find that in 1930 an Edmund J. holds the patent
for the manufacture of zinc sulfide. I find that in 1925
Edmund P. of Eastman Kodak holds many patents for film
processing. I get excited when I find that in 1929 Thaddeus J.,
who I assume is my great-grandfather, the one whose name
is etched inside the grasshopper weathervane on the roof
of Faneuil Hall, secures the patent for a new and improved
roof drain. After a few more fruitless hours I assume this
roof drain is the extent of the inventions in my bloodline.
Fifteen minutes before closing time on my third day I find it:

> *To all whom it may concern:*
> Be it known that I, Edmund T. Flynn, of
> Cambridge, in the county of Middlesex and State
> of Massachusetts, have invented a new and useful
> Life-Raft.

The problem was to keep the body above the waves.
The trick was to breathe only air. My grandfather's
patent was used by seven countries during both World
Wars. Thousands of heads floating above the waves.
I'll be damned.

from *another bullshit night in suck city*

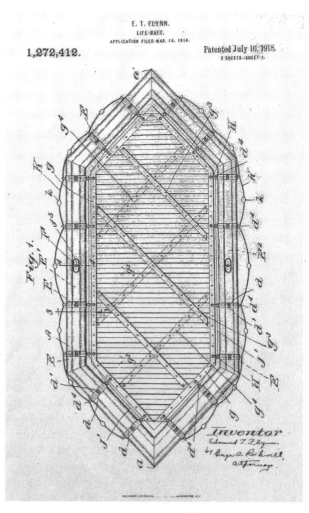

edmund flynn (my great-grandfather),
blueprint of his original patent for the
life raft, 1918

ROSCOMMON

It's one hundred degrees when I pull into Roscommon.
I find my father in the dayroom, with the rest. The woman
in charge of activities (Iris) asks my father if he knows
who I am. He looks at me blankly. Do you know who
Nicholas Flynn is? she asks. Nicholas Flynn? That's my
son. That's me, I say, and he turns and takes me in.
I have two sons, he tells me. I know, I say, I'm Nicholas.
The woman across from us recognizes me, and I recognize
her—her name is Mary. Mary rolls her eyes when my
father tells me my own name. You look like my cousin
Brenda, she tells me. Three other women are at my father's
table, I recognize them all—Dorothy, Josephine, Carol.
It's two in the afternoon, everyone gets popsicles, but
not my father (special diet, aspiration danger). I ask Iris
if we can put the DVD on the flat-screen, which is turned
up very loud. We turn off Oprah, slide the DVD in. I
point to the screen, That's De Niro, I tell my father, he's
playing you—my father looks confused. I remind him
about the time they met. O, yes, he says, I remember.
A few minutes later Paul Dano appears, lying in bed. His
voiceover tells us, *I'm just trying to wake up.* I look over
at my father, to tell him that Dano is me, but my father
has nodded off to sleep.

    I return the next morning, at ten o'clock, when
I know he will be awake. He is back in the dayroom. I sit
down next to him, ask, Do you know a Nicholas Flynn?
Tricky Nickie, my father says. He's my son. The television
is loud. I offer my hand, tell him to give me a firm
handshake. I'm your son, I tell him. O, he says. What's
your name? Nicholas Flynn, I tell him. You're Nicholas?
I ask Iris if we can turn down the television, but today
we cannot turn it down. We're about to have a sing-along,
Iris tells me. I set up my computer on the table in front
of my father and slide the DVD in. Iris hands out xeroxed
packets of songs, and the sing-along begins—*Birds are
singing, for me and my gal.* I pull the computer closer to us,
lean into my father, point to the screen. That's Robert
De Niro, playing you when you drove a taxi in Boston.
He's a hot-looking shit, my father says. Dressed well.
America has produced only three classic writers, De Niro's
voiceover tells us—Mark Twain, J.D. Salinger, and me.
I'm Jonathan Flynn. Everything I write is a masterpiece.

I repeat what De Niro just said, and my father nods. The other fourteen people in the room sing, *In love-land, for me and my gal*. I lean in closer, plug in my earbuds, try to put one in my father's ear, but he bats it away. What are you doing? he barks. We are put on this earth to help other people, Dano parrots, and a few moments later he gets punched in the face. I just got punched in the face, I tell my father, pointing to the screen. Seriously? my father asks. I point to each actor, say, That's Nick Flynn, your son. He says, Nicholas Flynn, that's my son. I say, I'm Nicholas Flynn, and my father glances at me. O, yes, he says. I point to the other actors as they appear—That's Jody, your wife. That's you. This is Al. O, yes, my father says, each time. *Five foot two, eyes of blue*, everyone but us sings. *Diamond rings and all those things*.

The season is
SUMMER

Many are in wheelchairs, one woman's hair is dyed bright red. *Has anybody seen my girl?* Now Olivia Thirlby is reading the letters my father sent me from prison. That's Jessica, I tell my father, and he says, Jessica? She was always kind, he says. Olivia reads, Punch drunk, dead drunk, mean drunk . . . . What is this? she asks. A poem, Dano tells her. *When Irish eyes are smiling*, our chorus sings. It's shit, Dano tells her, no one will ever read it.

The weather is
HOT and (a drawing of the sun)

This is you, I tell my father, you have been evicted from your apartment. You were sleeping in your cab, and now this is your first night sleeping outside. De Niro is in a library, writing a letter. The poor and the hungry are our constituents, De Niro's voiceover tells us. Then the library closes, and De Niro is in a coffee shop. That's you having a cup of coffee, I tell my father. Now? he asks. In the movie, I tell him. You have no place to sleep, you're going to have to sleep outside tonight. That's not unusual, my father tells me. *Tiptoe through the tulips*, the room sings. Bare feet, my father says. What? I ask. He's looking over at Iris, who is singing, *Tiptoe through the tulips*, her shoes kicked off. Beautiful legs, my father says.

The next holiday is
FOURTH OF JULY
(a drawing of a flag)

Now De Niro walks through the snow to the blowers.
Here's the blowers, I say. Behind the library, remember?
You're going to spend the night on the blowers. Recently?
my father asks. A few scenes later we are in the shelter.
This is Pine Street, I tell him. The Pine Street Palace,
he sneers, leaning in closer to the screen. Where is the
shelter kept? he asks. I look at the screen. Fake snow is
falling. You slept outside for a couple months, then you
went to the shelter. To get a bed. That's where you and
I will meet. That's nice, my father says. We watch for a
couple moments in silence. Our chorus sings, *You are my
sunshine, my only sunshine.* Where did you get this thing?
my father asks. You mean the computer? He looks back
at the screen. Is this the one in the South End? he asks.
Is it still open? It's still open, I tell him. Now Dano is
talking to De Niro through the mesh of the Cage. He
works at Pine Street, I tell my father, he's upset that his
father is staying there. I would think so, my father says.
Why? I ask. It's a tough situation, he says. These few
words are more than we have ever spoken to each other
about what those days were like for him, for us. You slept
in the shelter for a while, I remind him, then you slept
outside. That was bad, my father says, all bravado gone.
You make me happy when skies are gray. What was bad?
I ask. Sleeping outside, my father answers. But the shelter
wasn't exactly paradise.

When it's over I stand, close the computer, take
his hand. I have to be somewhere, I tell him. I'm already
pushing it. Where will you go? my father asks. Rhode
Island tonight, I tell him. I'm doing a reading. What will
I do? he asks. In his mind he's back on the streets, back
in the years he slept outside, I know this. You'll stay here,
I tell him. Lunch is coming. When? my father asks. Right
now, I say.

from *the reenactments*

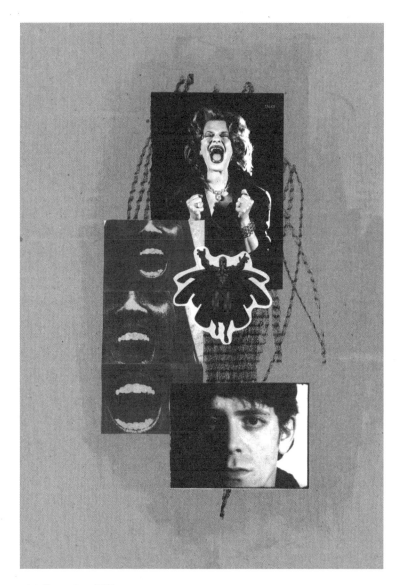

nick flynn, *lou*, 2011

zoe leonard, *tree + fence, out my back window*, 1998

I look in his eyes

        as he speaks, somehow

I'd learned to do that

        like a tree learns to

swallow barbed wire

from *another bullshit night in suck city*

THE DAY LOU REED DIED

It's not like his songs are going to simply
evaporate,

but since the news I can't stop
listening to him

on endless shuffle—familiar, yes, inside
me, yes, which means

I'm alive, or was, depending on when
you read this. Now

a song called "Sad
Song," the last one on *Berlin*,

sung now from the other side, just talk,
really, at the beginning, then

the promise
or threat, *I'm gonna stop*

wasting my time, but what else
are we made of, especially now? A chorus

sings, *Sad song sad song sad song sad*

song. I
knew him better than I knew my own

father, which means
through these songs, which means

not at all. They died on the same day,
what a perfect day, maybe

at the same moment, maybe
both their bodies are laid out now in

the freezer, maybe side by side, maybe
holding hands, waiting

for the fire or the earth or the salt
or the man—

if I could I'd let birds devour whatever's left
& carry them into the sky, but all I can do

it seems
is lie on the couch & shiver, pull a coat

over my body, as if it were all I had, as if I
were the one sleeping outside, as if it were my

body something was leaving, rising up
from inside me

& the coat could hold it inside
a little longer.

from *my feelings*

OBITUARY: JONATHAN ROBINSON FLYNN

JONATHAN ROBINSON FLYNN, the self-proclaimed "greatest writer America has yet produced," died on a Sunday morning at the end of October in Boston. At the time of his death he was living at Roscommon, the nursing home where he'd spent his last five years of his life. He was the subject of his son Nick Flynn's 2004 memoir, *Another Bullshit Night in Suck City*, which chronicled his father's life as an absent father, a bank robber, and a federal prisoner, as well as the five years he lived as what we now call "the working poor," sleeping in shelters and on the streets of Boston, working day labor. He made it off the streets with the help of several social workers and organizations, including Eileen O'Brien of Elders Living at Home, Jim O'Connell of Health Care for the Homeless, the Pine Street Inn, and many others. His success in getting off the streets is a model for the current Housing First movement, which has the potential to end homelessness in America.

Jonathan Robinson Flynn was born in 1929 in Scituate, Massachusetts, and always had a complicated and contentious relationship with his own father, Edmund Flynn, although Jonathan was proud that his father had, in response to the sinking of the *Titanic*, invented the life raft—the *Titanic* only had life-boats.

A ghostly, inscrutable, charming, frustrating, narcissistic, alcoholic, damaged, and damaging presence, Nick Flynn tried to understand his father in nearly all of his writing, especially in the subsequent memoirs *The Ticking Is the Bomb* and *The Reenactments*. Jonathan spent most of his life on the East Coast, between New Hampshire and Florida, often working on docks or on fishing boats in order to support his writing and his drinking. While serving time in federal prison it is likely he was subjected to CIA-funded torture experiments, which likely contributed to his later paranoia—Nick Flynn's *The Ticking Is the Bomb* chronicles this time in his father's life. After prison, he remained in Boston for the last 25 years of his life.

Being Flynn, the feature film based on *Another Bullshit Night in Suck City*, starring Robert De Niro as Jonathan Flynn, was released in 2012. Jonathan was impressed with De Niro's performance and enjoyed imitating De Niro ("You are me, I made you") as he taunted Paul Dano, his on-screen son.

At the time of his death Jonathan Flynn remained convinced he would win the Nobel Prize for "both storytelling and poetry." His one completed novel, *The Button Man*, remains unpublished. Along with his son Nick, he is survived by another son, Thaddeus, as well as a daughter, Anastacia.

For no good reason he outlived both of his ex-wives.

born 7 dec 1929, died 27 oct 2013, age 83, R.I.P.

my father & me, 1960

Stay, the bed is huge, we can share it.

Bewilderment
(& The Eternal Present)

I've come to believe that my only project, this go-round, is to get my feet on the ground—to land, in some way. But to land, it seems, I have to go through these periods of bewilderment, of unknowing. I could fake it, I'm good at faking it, maybe too good. I learned early on how to dissociate, it's like a switch I can simply flick off. I could easily fake sitting here, yet I'm actually here, sitting here, right in front of you. But if I haven't wandered in that wilderness, if I haven't followed the threads deeply into the psychic realm, then even my sitting here will be false.

rachel zucker talks with nick flynn,
commonplace (podcast), 2016

MINK DEVILLE PLAYS THE PARADISE
(BOSTON, 1978)

What follows is a story I've told many times, and if it works it's because it ends with me in jail. Sometimes I tell it as if I've never been set free, and then it works even better.

Some background: Legend has it that only a minuscule number of people bought the Velvet Underground's first album, but that each one of them went out and formed their own band—such was the reach of their influence, or so the story goes. I can think of no one who formed a band after buying Mink DeVille's first album. All traces of their influence, if there were any, are lost. Still, their debut album, *Cabretta*, from 1977, is a masterpiece, but most people have never even heard of it, or only vaguely if they have.

The story: I saw Mink DeVille at the Paradise when this album was still on display at the front of the record store in the mall, the mall a half an hour from my house. A worker there must have liked it, for it occupied that front rack for months, though it went unbought and unknown, at least in my hometown, except among my small gang of friends, and this in part was what attracted us to it. My friends and I were the only ones who knew how perfect it was, and each song ("She's So Tough," "Spanish Stroll," "Cadillac Walk," "Mixed Up, Shook Up Girl"—a handful more) was ours alone. Perhaps the appeal of the underdog was part of our devotion, for we were, or at least felt we were, misfits.

On the cover of that first album Willy DeVille's gaunt face stares out from an orange background in three-quarter profile, his cheekbones jutting like wings beneath his deer-in-the-light eyes, outsized eyes, junkie-gaunt, hair slicked back. *Cabretta* became the soundtrack to our last year of high school, and that same winter they played Boston, which seemed the center of a certain smoky bleary universe, and which it was easy to drink in with my brother's ID. We drove the hour in from the suburbs, and in that hour we drank, and this drinking continued in the club, so much so that I knocked over some tables every time I stood up, and I stood up at the beginning of every song, so I knocked over many tables, upended many drinks. We had a table in the front, and midway through the set Willy DeVille gestured once to me, for a sip of my beer, and I handed it up to him, and he tilted it to his lips, and passed it back.

Understand, we were kids stranded in the teenage wasteland of the suburbs, before it was pharmacologically transformed into the daydream nation of "the 80s", before traces of Prozac were reported in the drinking water, before we as a country decided to accept the unacceptable and watched as our children stepped over bodies sleeping on the streets on their way to school. Then Mink DeVille appeared, with their weird hybrid of punk discord and soul, a harmonic wail from a doo-wop street corner. It's odd to imagine it was once considered punk in any way, so distant from the hardcore that would soon become my breakfast of champions. Willy DeVille didn't sing politics like The Clash, he was clearly an anachronism, the last stop of innocence as Reagan's limousine rolled down Pennsylvania Avenue into the White House for the first time.

Willy DeVille had never threatened to change the world, but on that first album he was at least awake. Like any great art, it is both transforming and eternal, contains both matter and anti-matter, being and non-being, self and non-self—it embodies duality. And listening, it was clear that all us sleepwalkers could also awaken. We didn't know he was already strapping himself into his duct-tape time machine, flying backward into the land of nostalgia and string sections, into boogie-woogie and tin pan, so that when he disappeared he didn't exactly go, but he didn't exactly stay either. Always both coming and going— that was part of his greatness. He seemed to suggest he'd be back in a minute, like when a concert ends and we stand applauding and yelping. But it went on for hours, then years, and the lights never came up, the doors never opened. The word was he had moved to Europe, where they got him.

I said this would end with me in jail. Here I am. It is cold and they have taken my belt and coat and socks and the cell has a metal bed and cinderblock walls and a broken window. Snow falls on me as I try to sleep. My other friends are in adjacent cells, but we can't see each other. We can talk, but we are still drunk and what is said is not important. At some point in the night someone screams from another cell that he's fallen and cut his head. He is not one of us, wasn't in the car with us after the concert when we were pulled over and handcuffed and tossed in the back of separate cruisers. He screams for hours and hours it seems. The guards tell him to shut the fuck up. He screams that he's bleeding to death. We saw him carried in earlier and heard that he was on angel dust. After an hour of screaming he pries the toilet off his wall and smashes it against the bars, and water slowly begins to fill the cells. We don't have our shoes, remember, so if we step down our feet get wet. We all begin yelling, and the guards come, and they drag the screaming guy out, and bring him back hours later, his head shaved and stitched up, wearing a straightjacket. In the morning we are shackled together in a line and led into a van which brings us to a court where we will stand before a judge and be given fines. I am shackled to the screaming guy, who is still in his straightjacket. When we are finally set free we have to ask what town we are in, and we have to ask where our car ended up, and how to get to it.

from *the show I'll never forget*, an anthology,
edited by sean manning, da capo press, 2009

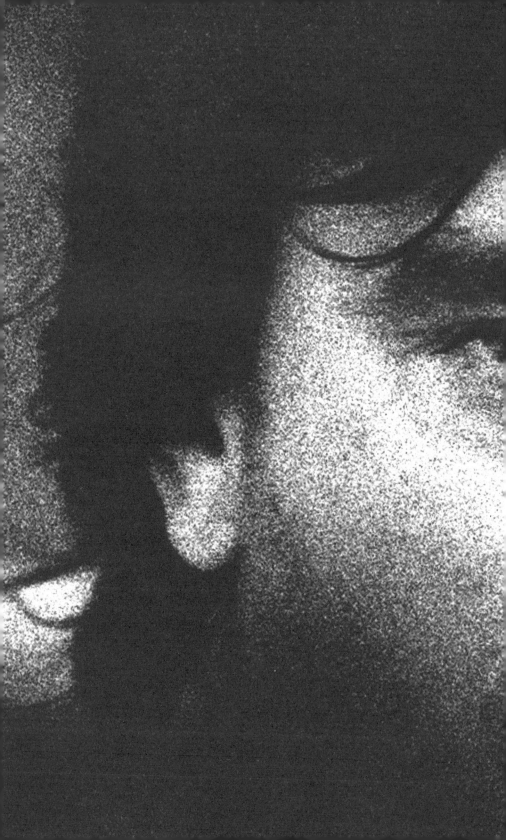

ON CRIME

I spent a lot of time on my own when I was a child. We
moved into the first house my mother owned when
I was five, and then we moved out when I was eight. In
those three years I was running around on my own a lot—
my mother was at work all the time. We lived in Scituate,
Massachusetts, near the center of town, which was called
the Harbor. I knew the backs of all the stores and I would
try to open all the doors. One time I found a metal grate
covering a crawlspace that ran under the bank. I could
pry the grate up and put my head into the hole. I was so
tiny that I could squeeze into the little hole. I came back
the next day with a flashlight. I crawled through the tunnel,
maybe it was an air vent, all the way to the end, where
there was a glass window with wire mesh embedded in it.
Maybe it was alarmed, maybe not. From there I could look
into the basement of the bank. I couldn't see any money,
but I imagined if I kicked my way in I'd find some money.

Scituate was a place where half the people went away when
summer ended, leaving their houses empty all winter.
Sometimes I'd break into those houses, it wasn't hard.
There was always a hidden key behind a pot or something.
I didn't take stuff, I'd just look around, maybe sit in a chair.

When I was seven I got caught shoplifting. I'd go into the
supermarket that my mother had worked in a couple years
earlier. She'd worked in the supermarket bakery making
donuts, she'd go in at five in the morning and sometimes
bring me along. I'd get to wander the aisles and eat anything
I wanted. We were really broke so this was a perk. She
stopped working in the supermarket when I was six, but I'd
still go in by myself after school. I'd pick up a plum and
start eating it. I'd put a bag of chips in my pocket, just walk
out. One day the manager stopped me and asked, What
are you doing?

My mother's second husband, John, was a Vietnam vet.
He was in a psych ward for a while, just before we met
him, but I didn't know that until years later. Cops began
showing up at our house the years he lived with us,
sometimes with warrants, sometimes not. I learned to tell
them that we hadn't seen him. I learned how to act around

the police very early on, that you don't look them in the eye, or give them any information, that they aren't your friends. When John moved in my mother was thirty-one and he was ten years younger. To me he was more like a wild older brother. He'd take whatever he wanted. He'd go to the lumberyard and steal wood to renovate our house, to build a bedroom for him and my mother. It was thrilling, it transformed the world into endless possibility. We were so broke, we had nothing. Suddenly, what we needed, we just took. In the summer he'd take us out fishing. We'd walk down the pier, find a boat with keys in it, and off we'd go. At Christmas he'd take me to the church field where they sold Christmas trees. We'd drag a couple trees we liked to the edge of the field, then come back later, after midnight, and throw them in the back of his pickup. After he left I continued to do this, to drive to the church after midnight, for years, then the next day showing up at my grandmother's, at my girlfriend's, with a nice tree.

A couple years later my mother had another boyfriend, Bert, who ended up getting busted for running the largest drug smuggling ring on the East Coast. My mother had gone out with him ten years earlier, when he was small time, just starting out, and then she went out with him again, ten years later, when he was big time. I knew what he was doing, even if my mother would never admit it. But it was obvious. I was seventeen, getting high all the time. Bert would disappear on "fishing trips" to South America, for three or four months. No one goes all the way to South America to fish, much less for three months. What's he fishing—whales? What is he, Ahab?

She ended up getting me a job with him. At first I just started out by unloading fish from the boats. It was mind-numbingly boring. I'd get high all day. Then I got promoted to being the electrician's apprentice, which I did for five years. We'd wire these fishing boats to make them suitable for long trips, with all this high-tech stuff on the inside, but make them look like normal fishing boats on the outside. The control center for this operation was at the electrician's house, which I also worked on. We called it the mother ship, it had a big radio tower in the yard. We knew we were being watched, photographed,

wiretapped—everything was being surveilled by the DEA.
One night my mother and I were eating dinner, we looked
up and there was Bert, on the nightly news, being led off
a boat in handcuffs. It was the biggest bust the DEA had
ever made. We showed up in court as a family even though
we weren't really a family. Character witnesses. It's good to
have kids in court. I wrote a letter to the judge. Before he
got busted he'd begun to run cocaine with small airplanes.
Then they started using coke. Then it all got really messy.
Then it fell apart.

I had a very romantic notion of crime before I started
working with him—I saw crime as a Robin Hood–type
thing. I thought it was a life outside the mainstream. But as
I got closer I saw that, in reality, it was deeply mainstream.
These guys, all they wanted to do was have a big car, a big
house, and live really upper-middle-class existences. They
did all this wild stuff just to have a big-screen tv. As I got
closer and closer it seemed less and less appealing.

I was sixteen when my father went to jail. We didn't talk
about him much before that. My mother had a warrant
on him and knew that if he came around he'd get arrested.
The warrant was over non-payment of child support. If
he was in town, he'd sneak over to my grandmother's, to
have a few drinks with her, and sometimes he'd leave some
inappropriate gifts for us, often something he'd stolen.
When I was little it was Steiff stuffed animals. Once it
was a puppy, but my mother refused to let me bring
it home, so it became my grandmother's dog. I didn't meet
my father until I was in my late twenties, but I got letters
from him for ten years before that. I have hundreds of
them, from when he was in prison and then after. He'd
done three-to-five years in federal prison for bank robbery
and got out in two.

from *crime,* an anthology,
edited by alix lambert, fuel publishing, 2008

ON ADDICTS

KAVEH AKBAR
. . . it seems to me
that you're more
interested in the
psychological
and cosmological
ramifications of
addictions, rather than
the literal experiential
narratives of what it
was like.

NICK FLYNN
All my friends
are addicts . . .

KA
Mine too.

NF
. . . and we all have the
same story, basically.
There was a time in my
life when I realized, in
horror, that every story
I told began with,
We were so fucked-up . . .

KA
Yeah!

NF
Every story. I could
have tattooed that on
my arm—"I was so
fucked-up, and then this
really fucked-up thing
happened." For a while,
longer maybe than it
should have, it was kind
of fun, how wild and
transgressive life could

be. Yet it was always
the same story. At some
point I heard myself
and thought, *There's*
something strange
about that.

KA
Yeah. One of the
beautiful, terrible things
about recovery is that
it disabuses you of any
sort of notion of how
singularly incredible
your particular addiction
narrative is, you know?

NF
And there is a beauty
to that as well, to
being disabused of that
notion. There's the
isolation of the addict,
and then there's the
unity of recovery. And
what unifies us is that
experience of eventually
reaching the last room—
one day you find
yourself there, in the
room with no doors,
and you say, *Oh, this*
isn't what I expected.
I thought there'd always
be another door.

kaveh akbar talks with nick flynn,
divedapper, 2017

Man with a Movie Camera, 1929, USSR, Directed by Dziga Vertov (pg. 30)

nick flynn, *oncoming*, 2005

MY JOKE

As I put the pipe to my lips

As I lift the flame to the glass

My joke

As the smoke fills me: *Say goodbye to*

Nick, even if

I am the only one in the room

& by the end I was always

The only one in the room.

from *my feelings*

hubert sauper, *nick flynn / after the crash*, 2007

ARIZONA DREAM

I don't know many Americans who've ever seen, or even heard of, the film *Arizona Dream*. It was made by the Yugoslavian director Amir Kustarica—he began it when there still was a Yugoslavia, but the war broke out during the shooting and half the crew was Bosnian and half was Serbian and quickly things got complicated. The shooting was shut down for several months, but it was somehow finished, and, according to my friends in Paris, it has played pretty much non-stop there, somewhere, for the past twenty years. I've never met anyone in Paris who hasn't seen it and who doesn't love it.

It's a great movie, strange and rambling, but it's possible that its cult popularity in Paris is due in large part to the fact that it stars Jerry Lewis, who for some reason the French are very fond of. It also stars Faye Dunaway. Lewis owns a car dealership, and he and Johnny Depp drive to Dunaway's place in the desert—I think Lewis and Dunaway, the characters they play, were married once, but I'm not positive. It's been a while since I've seen it—ten years actually. I know this because our daughter is now nine, and the last time I saw it my now-wife was pregnant with her.

I heard that one should travel before a baby is born, because once she arrives it will be harder. So I flew to Paris to see my pal Hubert. I had worked on his film

Darwin's Nightmare, which had been nominated for an Academy Award the year before. *Darwin's Nightmare* is a documentary about fish and guns that we'd shot around Lake Victoria, and I was thinking of writing something about it, and I wanted to ask Hubert some questions. The questions, I knew, were complicated, and his answers were elusive, and we got into a fight, which was unusual. I was jetlagged and hungry and before I got to crash for a few hours Hubert declared, *Tomorrow we fly!*

Hubert was just beginning what would become his next film (*We Come as Friends*), but at this point it was just an idea. The idea was to fly a small plane, an ultralight, all the way down the Nile. If *Darwin's Nightmare* was about globalization, this film would be about colonialization.

I first heard of *Arizona Dream* when I introduced him to my wife (Lili Taylor). It turns out that when Jerry Lewis and Johnny Depp pull up to Faye Dunaway's house in the desert, there is also a young woman there, and the woman is Lili Taylor. Maybe she's Dunaway's daughter, I forget. Vincent Gallo is also there, or maybe he came with Lewis and Depp. One of them has a plane, or they find a plane in the barn, an ultralight, just like the one Hubert planned to fly down the Nile. *Arizona Dream* was, in fact, where he got the idea. When he met Lili, at the release of *Darwin's Nightmare*, it was for him a sort of cosmic affirmation.

Three years later, Lili now pregnant, I woke up in Paris and Hubert hadn't answered any of my questions. We ran to the train, and I was desperate for an Advil. Hubert had stayed up all night re-watching *Arizona Dream*. Once we settled into the train, Hubert opened his laptop, and began playing his favorite parts. Vincent Gallo reenacting the airplane scene from *North by Northwest*, where a plane menaces Cary Grant in a cornfield, and he has to run from it, and throw himself into the dirt to avoid getting cut up. Gallo reenacts it all at a local talent show in a bar, a conceptual performance piece for the locals. Another scene is the one where Faye Dunaway goes up in the ultralight and crashes it into a tree. The last scene, which in my memory Hubert put on a loop, comes near the end of the film. Lili goes into the yard at night with a gun and shoots herself. In my memory Hubert played this scene over and over, and I was in some way paralyzed, unable to stop him.

It was like that scene in *Clockwork Orange*, the landscape flickering past the train windows.

When we got to the hangar it was a beautiful day. We rolled the plane out, Hubert did whatever one is supposed to do, and took off. I stayed on the ground, so when he made his first pass over the field I did my best Cary Grant imitation, or at least Vincent Gallo's version of Cary Grant. I walked casually at first, glanced over my shoulder, and as Hubert dipped the plane lower I began to run. He would come close, and I'd throw myself into the dirt as he passed over me. We did this a few times, which seemed to somehow heal the fight we were having, and then he landed.

I strapped myself into the passenger seat. An ultralight is not a big plane, it is, in fact, shockingly insubstantial. An aluminum frame, nylon wings, an engine, a propeller, a couple seats. A Plexiglas windscreen—a very Wright Brothers contraption. Taking off was thrilling, we could feel every blade of grass. Then the grids of farmland, the blocks of green, the blocks of brown. O there's a farmhouse. O there's a tractor. O there's the train we came in on. Once we were up high, Hubert passed me the stick. I flew for a while, rolling to the right, rolling to the left. It was completely possible I'd be part of this movie as well, that I'd be flying down the Nile with Hubert, looking for the film he was hoping to find. It could happen, so I should learn. After an hour or so we headed back to the landing strip. But something had happened in the sky while we'd been looking down. Now we were in the sky and something was happening in the sky. It was no longer blue—when did that happen? And the wind had picked up, so that the little plane was being buffeted—like when the pilot flicks on the fasten seatbelts sign. Turbulence, that's the word. A good time to get out of the sky. The first attempt to land the little plane failed—it was blown sideways off course, so Hubert simply pulled back on the stick and tried again. It was the same the next time, and the next. Now the sky was . . . not black, but not *not* black. Now the tops of the trees were swaying. The thing to do was to approach the landing strip sideways, to put the nose of the plane into the wind. We'd have less runway but at least we wouldn't be blown off course.

We circled back over the fields and as we came over the line of trees the plane went into a nosedive. If I could

I would slow this story down at this point, because that's what time did. The amount of time it took to fall was equal to the time it took to take the train here from Paris, equal to the time it took to watch the last scene of *Arizona Dream* over and over. Equal to the time we'd spent circling over the fields. The plane was speeding nose-first into the earth. At a certain point the entire Plexiglas windscreen was filled completely with green, the field rising up to meet us. I looked over at Hubert, he seemed utterly focused on pulling back on the stick, but it didn't seem to be attached. The nose of the plane was falling straight down, and we were in it. My wife was home with our child growing inside her. I felt an eerie calm.

Lili's character attempts suicide earlier in *Arizona Dream* as well, foreshadowing the end. But the earlier attempt was more *Harold and Maude*, more a performance of suicide than a bona fide attempt. During a dinner party she ties a rope around her neck and leaps from a balcony, but the rope is like a bungee cord, so she simply bounces up and down, up and down, while everyone else continues eating.

At the last second the nose tilted slightly up, but enough, enough for the plane to hit the earth hard and stumble through the tall grass for about ten feet before hitting a ditch and flipping completely over on its back. I found myself dangling upside down in my harness, kerosene pouring over me. Hubert unclipped himself and rolled away, likely imagining fire. It took me a few awkward moments to unclip myself and tumble the last foot to the earth. Once out I did like they do in the movies—I felt my body to see if anything was broken. Nothing was. I was giddy, I grabbed Hubert and hugged him. *We're fucken alive!* He pulled away. He had yet to secure funding for the next film, if they heard he crashed before he even left France it was over.

You must never tell anyone about this, he hissed.

performed live at *long story long*, industry, brooklyn, 2017

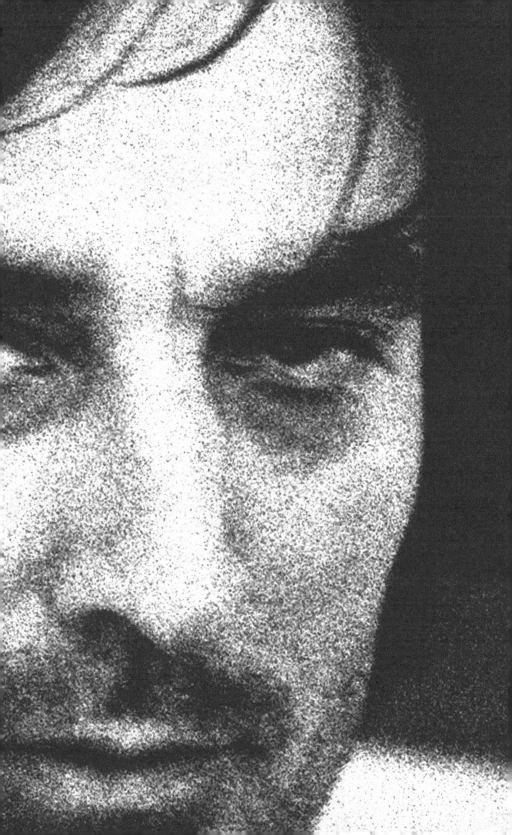

MANIFEST (O)

Our job as writers, as far as I can tell,
is to attempt to express what seems
inexpressible. The way we do this
(or one way) begins with a level of
absolute attention to the world, which
in and of itself is a difficult practice.
But it doesn't end there. Attention
merely leads us to the threshold of
the unknown, beyond which is where
poetry lurks.

Jung calls this place the *collective
unconscious*. Andrew Joron calls it
the *unsayable*. Lorca calls it *duende*.
Aristotle calls it *the mind in the act
of making a mistake*. Freud calls it
a *slip of the tongue*. Fanny Howe
calls it *bewilderment*.

The artist Bruce Nauman offers
this: *I think the point where language
starts to break down as a useful tool
for communication is the same edge where
poetry or art occurs. It is how the familiar
and the unknown touch each other that
makes things interesting.*

Nauman is talking about that
threshold between the conscious and
the subconscious realms. Instability
is one sign we have crossed the
threshold. We are no longer so sure
of what it is we are trying to say.

Yet, as the pre-Socratic philosopher
Meno asks: *How will you go about
finding that thing the nature of which is
totally unknown to you?*

bill schuck, *contrails* (detail),
his installation incorporating nf's poem
"her smoke (her trick)," 2005

HER SMOKE (HER TRICK)

A good waitress, I wait up for her
to come home, smoky

& exhausted, her feet
swollen, I wait in her bed. Purple shadows

cross the purple carpet, her television
makes Sherlock Holmes blue. He sees

evidence everywhere

of the man who last used this room, scrapes
mud from the floor into an envelope, rich

with lime, with ash fallen
from the factories in the east. I

doze. The tv turns to snow. Silently

she pulls off her black shoes, empties
her pockets. Next, her

genie trick, blowing smoke
into an empty juice glass,

cupping it with her palm until it slowly releases
up to the ceiling, the orange

tip of her cigarette a dying
ember. We

scatter her in the Atlantic, my brother & I, I
watch her sink, diffuse. I break off

another chunk of hash, impale it
on a common pin pushed up

through the cover of *Abbey Road*, set it on fire
under an upturned glass

& we take turns taking it in, our lips
to the tilted rim. Then we fall

back in our chairs, we never

talk about her, as if even her name
were ash

& might turn to paste in our throats.

from *some ether*

THE REPLACEMENTS

It's one of those days the radio tells us is dangerous to be alive, the air so thick it will kill you—an *air advisory* day. I bike from Brooklyn (where I lived and have always lived since landing in New York) over the Williamsburg Bridge to the Strand. It's my first summer in New York, I'm kneeling in the poetry section because that's where I go and when I go to get up I feel a woozy headrush—I'm overheated and really feel I'll collapse then and there and I know if I do they will simply roll me out onto the sidewalk and I will become part of the detritus. If I fall I will end up like Jimi Hendrix in the back of his last ambulance in Seattle—*Just another black junkie*, the EMT said—and they will drive around with me in the back, no rush, until we are all dead.

That was the day I realized that as far as New York was concerned (if New York could be imagined as a living being, like a hive) I was utterly and completely and immediately replaceable. New York didn't give a fuck about me unless it was able to suck out some energy—this was in fact what kept the city spinning. To New York we are all simply energy cells, especially the young, to be sucked dry and discarded. It is brutal and mean and the all glamour is empty, just like everywhere, except here the good guys and the bad guys dress exactly alike (hipsters) so you never know who you're talking to—rapacious capitalist? idiot savant? junkie trickster?

Here is the moment where I am supposed to say, *And yet* . . . but I'm not ready, not yet, for that. Maybe it's because we're all frozen in that first moment we stepped foot on the island, maybe that's why the fact that it hasn't noticed us, all these years, feels so stark. My first moment was when I was about five, we drove down from Massachusetts with a boyfriend of my mother's (David? Bert?) and went to Ripley's Believe It or Not!, where a man who had pulled out his own hair and eyelashes and fingernails had built from them a statue of himself. We went to the top of the Empire State Building, my mother cautioned that I would kill someone on the sidewalk below if I threw a penny down, that it would pass clean through his entire body (this was a lie). We went to the Automat for a futuristic lunch—tuna fish sandwiches and slices of pie behind little glass doors that opened when you put coins in.

But mostly what I remember was seeing a man sleeping on the sidewalk—it looked like one of his eyes was dripping out of his head. I swear I saw that.

A few years later my junior high social studies class took a bus down—a field trip—maybe forty of us. We went to the UN and to the newly opened World Trade Center and to see a magician (Doug Henning) in an afternoon show (Dustin Hoffman was in the audience and signed my program). I bought some magic cards and dropped them in the middle of Fifth Avenue and traffic had to stop and honk as I collected them all. I still have photographs from . that trip, each with a white border around it—now you can buy an app to re-create that white border "effect" if you want the photo to seem to come from the past, even though they all do anyway.

Ten years after that I drove my new pal Richard from Provincetown in my pickup truck back to his loft on Trinity Place—he'd fled a few months earlier to escape a nasty heroin habit and now we were back to pack up his stuff. We went out dancing to the Palladium and Area, places Richard had sometimes worked. My mother had died a couple years earlier and then Area closed and then the Palladium closed and then Richard died and by the time I moved to Brooklyn it was as if everything I knew or had known was slipping through my fingers—this is mostly what I feel and mostly what I've felt since I landed here, twenty years ago now—that I wander a city of the no longer here.

After my near-death experience in the poetry aisles of the Strand I was free of the illusion that New York gave a fuck whether I lived or died, whether I stayed or left—in this way New York began to correspond with my vague and ever-shifting concept of God. Whatever hole I left would be ignored, whatever apartment I vacated would be rented, whatever job I fled would be filled, all in an instant. If I was missed there were twenty poetry readings that night and twenty openings and twenty parties and twenty possible lovers that would all fill in whatever tiny void my passing left. What did I do with this sobering knowledge? I left, of course, many, many times. I tried Europe, Mexico, Africa, Vietnam, anywhere. Seattle? I tried—wrong ocean. The sun set *into* the ocean in Seattle and that was wrong— the sun is supposed to rise from the ocean, as it always did. I tried to leave, again and again, I would disappear for a week or a year and when I came back anyone I ran into on the street would simply look happy to see me (or avert their eyes, depending on how we'd left it) but it was as if we had spoken yesterday, not a year ago.

But there was something in this—in the fact that I would run into someone on the streets, each day, invariably, someone from a moment in my long history with the city, that began to add up, to something—some *texture.* Whenever I left I found myself missing precisely this— these random encounters. Each day, any day I venture out of my apartment, which is most days I wake up in New York, it will happen. I will, if I open my eyes, run into someone, randomly, either on the sidewalk or on the subway or in a coffee shop or a bookstore, someone from one of the decades of my life. Last week I ran into Marty outside a café in the West Village, he was talking to Sam about a play they might do together. Then I ran into Elissa outside a drugstore on Sixth, her daughter is now seventeen. I saw an ex on the A train platform outside Penn Station, standing with someone I imagined was her new lover. We were all heading downtown, we hadn't seen each other in years or spoken and we didn't that day, but we saw each other—we were still both alive.

Sometimes the seemingly random is not all that random. I go to an opening and there will be artists there I know, or I go to a reading and there will be writers. Which artist or which writer is the wild card, but there will always be at least one person there I will spend some time with—we will likely make a plan to get together later but even if we don't these few moments will be enough. I get around the city by bicycle, which makes these encounters either more or less likely, I don't know the math (I'm covering more ground but moving faster). My friends Doug and Tom have both mentioned seeing me ride past and not calling out for fear I would crash— were those random encounters, even if we didn't speak?

Last year I moved to Vancouver with my family for an indefinite period of time (it turned into seven months, but it could have been five years) and I knew even before I got there that I would never have a random encounter, not in Vancouver—since I knew no one there it would simply be impossible, and I was right. After I'd been in Vancouver for four months (four months without a random encounter), I flew back to New York for a reading, and stepping out of the taxi a block from my apartment I ran into Eli—Eli of Provincetown in 1999 and Rome in 2001—and it was as if we'd seen each other yesterday, as if I'd never left. It was at that moment I realized how important these encounters are to me, but I can't say why. I'm married, I have a child, all that is very, very good, yet there was an energy of first being in New York, the possibility, no, the certainty, that anything could happen, and that whatever happened would set in motion the rest of your life. It was before my life had started, I now see. I saw a beautiful girl one morning, I was on a corner in the Lower East Side, she came up and asked, *Are you looking too?* I knew she meant heroin, and if I said yes we would go and find it, but I didn't say yes. A couple years later I arranged to meet a blind date in a café near that corner, a place I'd write in for an hour on my way home to Brooklyn (I can't remember the name of it and now it is gone). As I walked in I saw a different woman at each table and it seemed any one of them could be my future. As it was the blind date and I stayed together for two years, and she did change my life. I run into her sometimes, it means something that we were together. New York will keep on spinning with or without us, but this is the part that isn't replaceable.

from *never can say goodbye*, an anthology, edited by sari botton, 2014

DEAR READER (OBLIVION)

I bought my ticket, I got on this train, it seemed
like I had someplace to be. The train, at some point,
went into a tunnel, one by one each car entered
the hole dynamited clean through the mountain.
It sounded like someone shuffling a deck of cards,
it sounded like when the projectionist falls asleep
before reel one ends, the acetate slapping the lens.
As the train entered the mountain some part of
me knew it would emerge again, in a few seconds
or a few minutes, but once inside that tunnel I
no longer cared if I ever came out the other side. In
that darkness I felt held, I didn't want it to end
If the train broke down, if it stranded me in the
darkness, I'd be blameless, like when I was a child,
coming home from the drive-in, my mother steering
us through the night, with me curled up in the
backseat, lost in my kingdom of sleep. I could have
stayed like that forever—my mother at the wheel,
the radio softly playing, Laura Nyro or the Standells
or Bobby Bland. I can open my eyes, even now,
and she will be there, we will still be together,
passing through dark streets—shadows of trees,
shadows of telephone lines, breaking up the sky
above us. When we pull into our driveway she will
carry me inside, put me into bed, either hers or my
own. I can't argue, maybe it's true, maybe I spent
too many nights in her bed, trying to hold her to
this earth, to quiet that voice inside her, calling
her back from the darkness. Sometimes she'd go
toward it, sometimes she'd get into her car after
midnight, I'd hear it start up, I'd hear her pulling
out, and later I'd hear her pulling back in, the gravel
under her wheels.
       I don't know how it is for you, but sometimes
still I walk through my days, fighting the urge.
Sometimes still I go on a little run, after so many
years of being clean. I take a hit, I make a call.
I knock on a door, someone answers, seemingly
happy to see me. I say *Yes* and *yes* and *yes.* I say, *Why
not?* I say, *Stay, the bed is huge, we can share it.* I
take a hit, make a call, a month goes by, I take
another, then maybe I take a hit every night

for a month—nothing much, a fistful of marijuana, and then I don't pick up for a year. Then I call you from the bathtub, we make a plan. Then I hang up and call someone else.

What I'm trying to say is that one December day I reached the age my mother had been when she passed into non-being (*goodnight nobody, goodnight mush*), when she finally stepped through the door she'd had her hand on all those years. I don't know, maybe some part of me decided I should try to find her—she couldn't have simply vanished. And so, after years without drugs, I took a hit. Then I took another. I was alone in Sleepy Hollow, it was always after midnight, maybe some part of me believed it was the only way I could find my way back to her, but I didn't know it at the time—it's not something I could have *ar-tic-u-la-ted*. Others speak of the fireworks that come, once they fall off the wagon— the police at the door, the four-point restraint—but I use the same way my mother did. For both of us there were no fireworks. A glass of wine, a tiny pill, the flame to the pipe, whatever we did, however we did it, it merely eased us into the night, into our private oblivion, our quiet desperation. We both always had jobs to go to the next day, we both felt bad at the idea of just not showing up. We always showed up, until one day she just didn't.

If anyone asked, I'd say that I hadn't had a drink in years, which was true, but I'd add that I sometimes took a hit of pot. I wasn't pretending to be sober, not exactly, but I wasn't saying I was out again either—I was *min-i-mizing* it. Then, after two years of getting high again, off and on, the voice inside began to murmur, softly at first, almost like an echo off a distant cliff, that everything would be better if I were dead. The suffering, my own and the suffering I was causing, would end. I brought myself to her door, I put my hand upon it, a voice just on the other side, all I had to do was push it open, step through. I knew I would meet her there. I knew we could stay like that forever.

from *The Ticking Is the Bomb*

HERE COMES THE SUN

In 2006 I was coming out of an extended trip through what I can now only call a spiritual wasteland. The first line from Dante's *Inferno* had been rattling around inside me— it seemed that I, too, had come to the middle of my life and found myself in a dark wood, having lost my way.

The woman I had been with for two years proposed, gently, that we either begin thinking about having a child together or begin thinking about going our separate ways. There was no threat in her voice; she preferred we go together into this uncharted territory, but it would be all right if I needed to be lost for a while longer.

I had always imagined I would be a father one day— but that day had yet to come. I wanted to be ready, and yet it seemed I never was—not quite.

Lili and I had both been in other relationships over the years and now we were in this one, and it was good. There was no reason not to have a child, except for the mindbending enormity of it. I'd always kept my own apartment, I'd never actually lived with a woman before, yet Lili and I had spoken of it on the first night we spent together. But the chasm between talking about something and actually committing to doing it can be great. Some days we stared across this chasm at each other, wondering if it was really right this time.

As we circled around the idea of having a child together, I was in the midst of working on a book. It had begun two years earlier as a meditation on the Abu Ghraib prison photographs and had transformed into an attempt to unravel why these photographs had snagged so firmly on my unconsciousness and deeply unsettled me. It was the bewilderment of waking up, my hand on Lili's belly, as the fine points of waterboarding were debated on public radio.

It's possible that, for me, talking about torture was easier than talking about my impending fatherhood, the idea of which, some days, sent me into a tailspin. Some people would tell me that once the baby came I would feel a new love, a love like I have never felt before. Hearing this, I'd smile and nod, but it made me uneasy. What if I didn't feel this love? I'm sure it can't happen to everyone, and that those who don't feel it simply don't talk about it. What if I turn out to be one of them? What if I feel it one day and don't the next?

In the summer of 2007 the due date (4 January) was an estimate, a long way away. By Christmas the doctor would tell us that she could come any day now. That summer she was already manifest, her hand waving against the tight skin of Lili's belly. But to me, it was all still deeply abstract. One day, soon, she would make her way into this world, she would open her eyes and breathe and cry. Would she suddenly become real to me? Would something heretofore unknown bloom inside my body?

At that moment it felt like I was on the slow ascent of a rollercoaster, the car climbing the rickety hill, just before the fall. And so, when I was not reading transcripts from Abu Ghraib, I was reading what I could about children. That summer I flew to Istanbul to meet some of the Iraqis depicted in the now infamous Abu Ghraib photographs. I was invited to be a witness to the gathering of testimonies by the lawyer who was putting together a criminal case against two American companies which had allegedly profited from torture. I flew to meet the lawyer, the ex-detainees, and their translators when Lili was five months pregnant.

One of the ex-detainees was the naked man being dragged on a leash by Lynndie England. Amir is the pseudonym given to him by Physicians for Human Rights, which examined him and corroborated his injuries and his story. During the week I spent with Amir there was a moment in his story when the only way to tell us what happened was to show us what they did to his body. He pushes back from the table and stands—they hung me this way, he says, and raises his arms out to his side as if crucified in the air. The lawyer shakes her head slightly. And what happened next? she says softly, and he lowers his arms and sits.

At first, before the baby was even here, when she was still in Lili, there was the fear that I wouldn't show up, for the birth or the aftermath. Or that I'd be there, but not there, a hologram of a father. My father, after all, had missed both my birth and my brother's, claiming car trouble both times, though he owned a car dealership. What if I had car trouble? There was also the fear that one or the other would die during childbirth. Did that still happen? But this fear was merely a mask, for then I could vanish into a hotel room, live out my days behind a closed door. This was a thought that passed through my mind. The next moment I was holding Lili's leg as the baby's head crowned. After what felt like another hour of screams and breathing she slid out like a seal.

Still wet, they moved her to Lili's arms—that was the first thing. Then we took a picture. That was the second thing. Then the baby was brought back down to Lili's feet, then I was handed a knife and directed to cut the umbilical cord. To make me feel a part of what was happening. I cut it, and I felt a part.

Soon our house would be filled with turtles, elephants, monkeys. All plastic, I don't know where it even comes from—China, I guess. I hear there are entire cities in China that make just one thing. *One day, Maeve, I will take you to the city of tiny elephants.* We named her Maeve.

One morning, months later, Maeve opened the bathroom door by pushing a tiny elephant against it. I'd never even thought of opening a door with an elephant. Neither had she, apparently, but now she did it, again and again, laughing each time. I found a gorilla on the pavement a few days later and brought it home, but a week later saw it on the pavement again, as if it were escaping.

In Istanbul, while collecting testimonies, we asked each ex-detainee to describe the room where his torture took place. Each man looked around him. It looked like this room, each responded. There was a table, there was a computer. What did the person who tortured you look like? was the next question, and the detainee would look at me, then at the artist, the only two white men in the room, and either point to him or point to me. He looked like him, was the answer.

One evening, Amir asked if I had children. I've been asked this question for years, whenever I travel, and I've been looked at with something like pity when I've answered no. My first child will be born in January, I told Amir. A girl. He narrowed his eyes and smiled, as if I had just come into focus.

Last night there was a lunar eclipse. I held Maeve up to the window to see it. I told her about the sun, about the Earth, about the moon, about the eclipse. I said: "You are the sun, I am the moon, I circle around you." I held her head like a sun, and we moved around the room singing "Little darlin', it's been a long, cold, lonely winter," until she stopped crying and fell asleep.

One day, recently, I flew to Indiana, and what did I find? A hotel room. A street where no one knew me. I knew not one person would come up to me on the street and ask, How's the baby? In Indiana I forgot, for the first time, for moments at a time, that I had a child that I loved. It's been two years since she arrived—"two," she can say it now, when asked how old she is. Two.

Before she came, if I tried to visualize her, I'd always end up back on that rollercoaster, in a broken-down car climbing a rickety hill, this tiny baby at the apex. As I'd reach her, as I'd take her in my arms, the car would begin its inevitable descent, then drop into freefall. Part of my fear was that as we fell I wouldn't be able to hold on to her, that she would fly out of my grip—I couldn't imagine that she could simply fall with me, safe in my arms.

published in *the guardian*, 2010

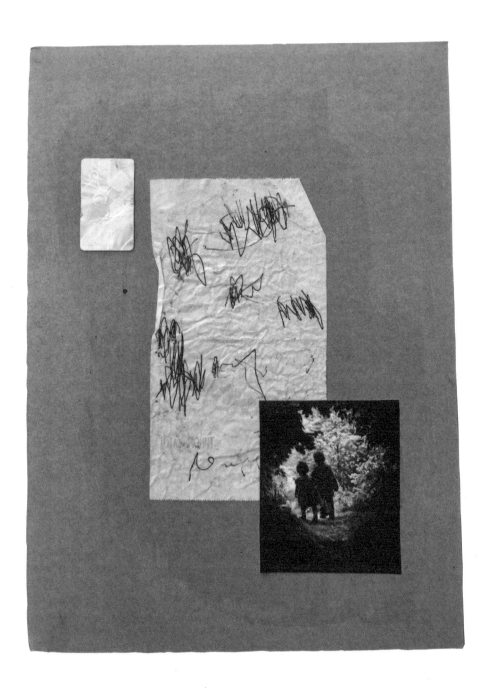

nick flynn, *fairy tale*, 2012

TAKEN

I once rode in a car through Paris while
a woman I barely knew read a poem
into my ear—*Apollinaire? Villon?* It was
a cabaret performance she'd do & she
offered to do it to me.

Each word vibrated inside my head.

For years I'd tried to read Rilke, yet
failed—what I mean is that I didn't get
Rilke. One night I read the *Duino Elegies*
out loud to my then-girlfriend—by the
end we got it.

A poem, I realized, could do what roots
do—cling to darkness, search out hidden
rivers, feed the visible world . . .

from the foreword to nick flynn's poetry selection
for *provincetown arts*, 2014

WHAT IS THE WIND?

After my daughter was born, twenty-one months ago now, I sent out a photograph of her to several friends, wearing one of those little hats they give out in the hospital to keep a baby's tiny head warm. Under the photo I wrote her name, weight, day and time of birth. *Everyone is fine*, I wrote. Until one day I looked at the photograph closely and couldn't identify the room it was taken in—it seemed to be someone else's kitchen. This was confusing, since we hadn't really traveled far, if anywhere, since she'd been born. Looking closely, I realized it was not only someone else's kitchen, but someone else's baby. It took a while to realize what had happened: A friend I hadn't seen in years had a child around the same time and had sent me an announcement. I'd dragged her child's photo onto my desktop, and apparently, I'd been sending that one out. It's possible that I even sent my friend a photograph of her own baby, claiming it was mine. I never bothered to tell those I sent the wrong photo to about my mistake. Some of the announcements had gone out to former girlfriends, for it seemed they should hear from me that I'd become a father, as unlikely as that might seem to them.

For a couple years before deciding to have a child, my life was, I'd tell anyone I got involved with, *complicated*. What I meant was that I was sleeping with a handful of other women and would likely continue sleeping with them. I guess it's called *dating*, though I never felt very good at it. I even, briefly, developed what some (not all) called a "reputation"—there might have been some truth to it. But, in my defense, during my "run," in an attempt to be honest, I'd tell anyone who was considering spending the night with me that I was in no shape to see anyone, not fully. To some this seemed enough, for a while, before we'd drift apart. Others tried to force the issue, to little result.

It was true, I really was in no shape to see anyone. In the past I'd experienced long stretches of monogamy, year upon year, which I preferred, the calm of it, but I was now out of a long-term relationship. I was also just past the age my mother had been when she shot herself in the heart (42), and fast approaching the age my father had been when he walked into his first bank and robbed it (a decision which would, in part, lead to his years of homelessness). It felt, sometimes, as if all the dark energy of my family history was roiling inside me, desperate to find purchase. I'd been through rough patches like this before, and at those times the only purchase I could find (outside of drugs) was through sex, which I knew was dangerous—sex (at least for me) is complicated enough, without trying to make it about anything other than what it is—ideally, the possibility of the deep pleasure that can come from two bodies coming together, gently or thrashingly or one transforming into the other then back again. Nothing more, nothing less. This is what I needed at that moment in my life, I told myself, I told anyone who asked.

After a couple years of this "dating" I narrowed my complicated life down to two women—which felt to me like progress. One I'll call Anna, the other I'll call Inez. The only trouble was that I had fallen in love with them both. In my mind (or perhaps simply in the reductive light of retrospection), one was light, one was dark. One was day, one was night. One I'd see in public, one I'd see in private. One was a self-proclaimed "drunk" (like my mother, like my father, like me), one was not. In some ways it was exhilarating, to be in love with two women, yet as it skidded along, with no end in sight, it became clear that I was merely, and willingly, moving deeper into that rough patch. Yet, somehow, it never felt scattershot, or unfocused, or careless. When I was with one, or the other, I felt fully there, which is perhaps merely a testament to how lost I'd become, without even knowing it. It was only in the in-between moments, when the phone was silent, or driving from one to the other, say, when I sensed that it couldn't be sustained, that it wasn't real, that one day, soon, I'd have to choose. Or, more likely, that one or the other would choose for me. I was spending a lot of time then in upstate New York—Rip Van Winkle country—the roads I was driving were always dark, darker than I ever remember driving through. I sensed that if I shut off my headlights I could simply vanish into this darkness.

I'd grown up with a mother who might have liked it if I had been able to heal her, at least this is how it often seemed. And so, for a long time, this became for me what love was, what it meant. I carried this (mis)conception, unaware, into every relationship—it was the air I breathed. My mother would eventually commit suicide when I was away at college, and I would go on to be in one relationship after another, some long term, some very brief. My mother's death was, inevitably, some part of what was going on with every woman I was with—and so it was with Anna, and so it was with Inez.

At some point (whether true or not), it seemed that Anna was working through some sort of damage (isn't everyone?). At that moment I knew my role, I knew what I was supposed to do. It made sense for a while, but in the end, it is likely precisely because of how I handled it, how I switched to autopilot, that determined that it wouldn't, couldn't, work out—it became too mired in my past experiences of trying, and failing, to save my mother. If Inez was working through her own damage (aren't we all?), she made it clear, from the beginning, that she'd be fine with me or without me. My presence wouldn't save her, my leaving wouldn't destroy her. It took a long time for me to become comfortable with it, this naming something as love which didn't hang on disaster.

After two years of the ever-increasing chaos of being in love with both of them, Inez made a proposition— the time had come to make a choice as to whether or not we would try to have a child together. The directness, her clarity, the weight of it, became a pinpoint of light in the distance that I somehow (grace?) chose to move slowly toward. The fact that she was ready to say goodbye, blamelessly, if I wasn't able to turn toward that light, and that she would be fine either way, made it clear that it was my choice. It also seemed clear to her that whatever it was I was struggling with has very little to do with her. I'd tried my whole life to save my mother from herself, and failed, in the end. Inez made it clear that our deciding to have a child together had nothing to do with saving her—it was simply about moving forward, together.

By making this choice, I of course had to say goodbye to Anna.

I'm no expert (clearly) but it does seem that some of us, men and women alike, use our past turmoil, cling to it, drag it out every year, around Christmas, say, wrap it around our bodies like a moth-eaten coat. I would call this a reenactment of damage. Say your mother died around Christmas (mine did), a long time ago now, and every Christmas her death starts to roil through you again, and maybe you go to your attic and take out the box with her photographs and letters and get lost in it for a while. And when you come down from the attic you are visibly shaken, and this can lead those so inclined to hold you a little closer, to comfort you. The tears you are crying are real, or real enough, though the tears you cry at an AT&T commercial are also real. But this reenactment of the trauma is perhaps the opposite of finding a way to embody the trauma, which might be another way of saying to *integrate* the experience into your everyday life, so that it no longer pulls the strings, makes you dance. But to embody, one must have a body. Sometimes, for many years, I'd borrow someone else's body for a while, put myself inside her, if only for a few minutes, or a few nights, until I could find, or find a way to enter, my own.

In a poem I wrote a long time ago, a semi-autobiographical "I" tells the story of a mother's death to a woman, and as "I" tells it "I" begins to cry, and the woman holds "me," as I know she will.

> Once
> upon a time, *let's say*, my mother stepped
>
> inside herself & no one
> could follow. More than once
>
> I traded on this, until it transmuted into a story,
> the *transubstantiation of desire*,
>
> I'd recite it as if I'd never told anyone,
> & it felt that way,
>
> because I'd try not to cry yet always
> would, & the listener
>
> would always hold me.

This poem is, in part, an attempt to shine some light on a way the stories we tell about ourselves, about our tragedies, can become packaged, somehow, contained. Yet there is, of course, a price for this. Packaging one's tragedies risks becoming, of course, grotesque in some way. For me the price became untenable, at some point, in that it contributed to my already slowly eroding sense of integrity. And so began the long daily practice of not doing that, of not letting a packaged story substitute for a genuine, if fucked-up and uncomfortable, emotion. The short story is that twenty years ago I quit drinking, got into therapy, settled down, became a worker among workers—the usual mundane paths trod by millions. Years went by, and then I found myself back at the beginning—lost, in love with two women, trying to save one, one who never asked me to save her and, in all likelihood, resented the way I was projecting my damage upon her.

If such a thing as momentous as deciding to be a father is to be a conscious decision (though I sense there are some who give it less thought than taking off a glove), then how does one decide such a thing? Do I believe that love can heal? I've written a memoir, *The Ticking Is the Bomb*, which is, in part, about how lost I was, nearly a vapor, and how deciding to have a child grounded me, or set me on the road to grounding myself, for the first time in my life. I don't think it was Inez who grounded me—it was this thing we did together. Committing to becoming a parent with someone is, for most of us, I assume, a fairly radical before and after. It all carries forward, but there is a threshold crossed. Here I am. Here we are. Plus one. Amazing. Somehow our child got the best of each of us, it seems. Having a child can be healing, I suppose, but I'm reluctant to even put that burden on her. Many people freak out when the child comes. For me it was a beautiful hallucination, at least for the first few sleepless months. And now it's just beautiful. But as far as healing, it was more the things I had to do to psychically prepare myself for her coming that healed me, if I am healed. I got back into therapy, began meditating every day, cleaned up. And now I feel lucky, that I can see her as a miracle, daily. Mostly. The moments I can't see the miracle she is I think of as thresholds into those parts of myself that are still, or might be still, damaged. The thing about damage is that if you can lead someone right to it, like a sleeping bear, point to it, say, *Shhhh, don't wake him*, then it likely is already toothless. At least for the winter months. Come spring everyone is damaged, all over again, whether they talk about it or not. It's just the world waking up. It's the sap running through the trees, it's the ice starting to thaw. Whatever damage has been sleeping is now awake, once more. True damage is not merely a reenactment of past turmoil, but part of nature, embodied somehow. That's why it's a good idea to stretch out each morning, if just to be aware of where in your body the damage is lurking today. I now think of it as a daily practice, which is the original meaning of the word *catharsis*—you wake up every morning in your same skin, and then do those things you have to do to find your best self. Some days it works better than others. Here I am, married, or nearly married. I have a child with the woman I live with—Inez. We are happy. Our child is happy. I am happy. Damaged happy? Maybe, but mostly just happy. I've asked Inez if she thinks that her love healed me and she just shudders. She has never seen this as her role, even though she radiates kindness, forgiveness, and generosity of spirit. But heal me? I would never want her to even attempt it. It seems to me, at this point, that it is up to me to attempt to heal myself, daily, and to bring that better self to her bed each night. Those are the good days. To heal me was never her job, nor do I think it is possible. Though there were times, which I now mostly attribute to laziness or fear, that I hoped she could.

This morning I hold my daughter as she stands on the windowsill, looking out onto the street below. A cold wind blows in on us, and she tilts her face into it, laughing. *What is the wind?* I ask her, and she points to the sky and says, *Trees.*

published in *elle / uk*, 2010

ROCK 'N' ROLL SUICIDE

In thinking about sex, drugs, rock 'n' roll and poetry, I'll
start by riffing off a Robert Duncan quote:

> "I want to compose a poetry with the meaning
> entirely occult, that is – with the meaning contained
> not as a jewel is contained in a box, but as the inside
> of a box is contained in a box."

*. . . meaning contained not as a jewel is contained in a box,
but as the inside of a box is contained in a box—*

To me this is a Zen koan, the idea that it is the emptiness
of the bowl that makes the bowl, that without the
emptiness there is no bowl. The idea that the self is only
made up of non-self elements (no flower without rain,
sunshine, dirt, worms, clouds, etc.).

But how does this connect to poetry? Poetry deals with
white space, it contains (or attempts to contain) the tension
of all that is unsaid, it pushes against the unknown . . .

Duncan again: "I want to compose a poetry with the
meaning entirely occult . . ."

Here is a definition of the *occult* (from Wikipedia):

> The *occult* (from the Latin word *occultus*
> "clandestine, hidden, secret") is "knowledge of the
> hidden." In common English usage, *occult* refers
> to "knowledge of the paranormal," as opposed to
> "knowledge of the measurable," usually referred
> to as science.

Knowledge of the hidden: Duncan wanted to not simply
push against the unknown, but to access, through poetry,
knowledge of the hidden. Knowledge of the hidden does
seem to be in the basic job description when applying to
be a poet, but for me, I have to be careful: the hidden is
a place to visit, but I have no desire to pack my bags and
move there—I need to always keep one hand on the earth,
to remind myself I exist.

As for *knowledge of the measurable*: any good scientist will admit that our knowledge of the measurable represents only a tiny sliver of the universe—nearly everything, still, is unknown . . .

But how does all this connect to sex & drugs & rock 'n' roll?

It has been pointed out that sex & poetry & rock 'n' roll need repetition, but I'd argue that, if you're someone like me, when you apply the concept of repetition to drugs, bad things happen. This is when someone like me enters the shadow realm, which has its own importance (transgression, the doors of perception, all that) but in the end it always seems to become mind-numbingly repetitive.

In the end, like mission creep, it reveals its lack.

Rock 'n' roll is, like drugs, essentially, about disruption— this is the good part. Think of Greil Marcus's extended riff on the Sex Pistols, *Lipstick Traces*—subtitled *A Secret History of the 20th Century*—it hopscotches across the art movements of the last hundred years that destroyed everything that came before, from Nijinsky's *Rite of Spring* to Dada to the Situationists to punk rock.

Marcus quotes Pete Townshend in his intro:

> "When you listen to the Sex Pistols, to 'Anarchy in the UK' and 'Bodies' and tracks like that, what immediately strikes you is that *this is actually happening.*"

This sort of distills Marcus's argument for the whole book, that the destruction was necessary & came at moments when the dominant culture was dead & needed to be shocked back into life, so we could know—feel— again that *this too is actually happening.* This, in the end, is the essence of Buddhism, isn't it? Look around this room: *This too is actually happening* (even if it seems I'm not in the room with you).

Speaking of mission creep, after the Abu Ghraib photographs were leaked (by a whistleblower / hero named Joe Darby), it was revealed that the U.S. Military (or the CIA), in

a pamphlet or a memo or something, suggested using
music as a form of torture—they'd blast Britney Spears &
Metallica, but found that country did the most damage—
"Achy Breaky Heart" (the Billy Ray Cyrus hit), turned
out to be especially harmful, or effective, depending upon
where you stood:

> *And if you tell my heart, my achy breaky heart*
> *He might blow up and kill this man . . .*

> *Or you can tell my eyes to watch out for my mind*
> *It might be walking out on me today*

Here's a type of disruption: *Tell my eyes to watch out for my
mind.* "Achy Breaky Heart" reminds me of this passage
from Hart Crane's *The Bridge*:

> *The phonographs of hades in the brain*
> *Are tunnels that re-wind themselves, and love*
> *A burnt match skating in a urinal.*

A turntable in hell caught in an endless loop, skipping
(more repetition). At this moment in Crane's poem we
are, like in "Achy Breaky Heart," in some sort of psychic
breakdown—it is night, we are underground, in a tunnel
(the New York subway, to be exact)—this is where many
poems come from, this is where poets live: nighttime,
shadows, dreams, darkness, walking with the devil. Robert
Johnson sings:

> *Early this morning*
> *When you knocked upon my door*

> *And I said, "Hello, Satan,*
> *I believe it's time to go."*

Hello, Satan. I assumed when the Abu Ghraib photographs
were released that it would be a disruption, violent, yes,
but that America would eventually break open in some new,
healthy way—but I was wrong. When ASCAP heard about
Britney & Metallica & Billy Ray being used to torture
detainees in Abu Ghraib, they tried to sue—not because
they didn't want the songs used to torture people, but for
the royalties. The suit went nowhere—the Bush White
House claimed state secrets.

After I heard that, I wrote a poem where I imagine a U.S. soldier playing Modest Mouse in Abu Ghraib—*And we'll all float on okay okay.*

Here are three excerpts from the poem:

WATER

>   before modest mouse capt'n what
>   was the world, what was the world
>
>   before pavement?
>
>   before I was nothing I was silence before
>   before I was here I was no one
>
>   the radio one day it made me of air
>   a soundtrack to walk down these halls
>
>   *we'll all float on okay okay*
>   *we'll all float on okay*

>   ~

>   they scream my lieutenant he calls it a song
>   I want them to sing he says louder
>
>   I wish you could hear the soundtrack we play
>   for hours & naked they dance
>
>   I take out my camera I capture the sound
>   at first it was weird then it wasn't
>
>   before there's a song there's a day it just isn't
>   before there's a photo it's dark
>
>   *& we'll all float on okay okay*
>   *& we'll all float on okay*

~

capt'n this morning six were found hanging
in a room made completely of air

they knotted their blankets their blankets dissolved
& their necks stretched to the floor

& yesterday capt'n thirty stopped eating
I forget the words to this song

we feed them with tubes their vitals are good
it helps to think it's a game

& we'll all float on okay okay
& we'll all float on okay

ASCAP has, so far, not attempted to sue me. Gil Scott-Heron
updated "Me & the Devil Blues" a year or so before he died:

Me & the Devil
Walking side by side
And I'm gonna see my woman
'til I get satisfied.

We all know about Gil Scott-Heron's final days, walking
with the devil, a blowtorch and a crackpipe by his side.
In the original version, Robert Johnson had proposed
"beating" his woman till he's satisfied, which is, or course,
much darker than merely "seeing" her. Duende can
contain both dark & light, a life force or a death force,
depending on how you look at it or where you're from.
Yet, a sliver of this dark energy is somewhere in every
good poem—poems are, after all, nothing but a
crossroads—with each step, with each word, a world
of what-if.

And we all know about Gil Scott-Heron's final days,
walking with the devil, a blowtorch by his side . . .

Here's a poem about my blowtorch:

PHILIP SEYMOUR HOFFMAN

Last summer I found a small box stashed away in
my apartment, a box filled with enough Vicodin
to kill me. I would have sworn that I'd thrown
it away years earlier, but apparently not. I stared
at the white pills blankly for a long while, I even
took a picture of them, before (finally, definitely)
throwing them away. I'd been sober (again) for some
years when I found that box, but every addict has
one—a little box, metaphorical or actual—hidden
away. Before I flushed them I held them in my palm,
marveling that at some point in the not-so-distant
past it seemed a good idea to keep a stash of pills
on hand. *For an emergency,* I told myself. What
kind of emergency? What if I needed a root canal
on a Sunday night? This little box would see me
through until the dentist showed up for work the
next morning. Half my brain told me that, while
the other half knew that looking into that box was
akin to seeing a photograph of myself standing on
the edge of a bridge, a bridge in the familiar dark
neighborhood of my mind, that comfortable place
where I could somehow believe that *fuck it* was an
adequate response to life.

. . . contained not as a jewel is contained in a box,
but as the inside of a box is contained in a box—

This too is actually happening.

a talk given at awp, for the panel "sex, drugs & rock 'n' roll,"
curated by beth bachmann, 2016

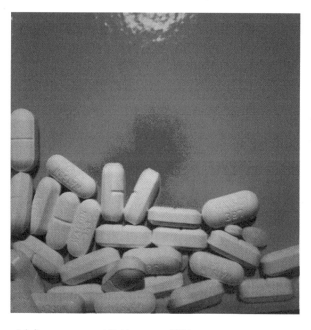

nick flynn, *every addict has one*, 2014

SOME (UNSTABLE) NOTES
ON THE IDEA & USES OF
THE EXTREME IN POETRY

1. Not every act of writing is extreme.

2. Like everything else, the idea of the extreme in poetry is on a continuum— if on one end is, say, *love*, then *death* could be on the other end.

3. Some poems are not on this continuum—they are on other continuums. These poems are more engaged with form, or sound, or silence, all of which can also contain elements of the extreme.

4. All lyric poems are extreme if the poet writes them with the awareness that they will one day die.

5. A poem does not have to end in death to be extreme, just as not all poems that end in death are extreme.

6. Death, in and of itself, is not extreme—neither is suffering.

7. Death is either simply the end of life or part of life or a threshold to eternity, depending upon your belief system.

8. All belief systems are subject to revision, like everything else.

9. Is it more extreme to believe that everything that lives is holy, or that there is only one god?

10. Descriptions of nature are not generally extreme, except for volcanoes, floods, plagues, etc.

11. Eco-poetics, though, can hover on the edge of the extreme—these poems engage with—and sometimes touch—the coming apocalypse.

12. That the apocalypse has been coming for a long time (see Blake) does not make it any less immanent.

13. *The Texas Chain Saw Massacre* is no more extreme than, say, *The Iliad* or *The Book of Revelation*.

14. In one section of the *Book of Revelation* (also known as the Apocalypse), seven bowls are poured onto Earth. The second bowl turns the sea to blood and everything within it dies. The third bowl turns all fresh water to blood. With the pouring of the fourth bowl, *The sun scorches the earth with intense heat*.

15. Certain locations—prisons, wars, burning buildings, sinking ships— are by their nature extreme, but it is still necessary to find tension within those structures to become a poem.

18. Sometimes on a beautiful nothing morning I'll listen to Iggy Pop, who wakes up parts of my brain in ways which might be considered extreme.

16. The extreme without tension is simply a wail.

17. Aimé Césaire, in *Notebook of a Return to the Native Land*, offered this: *. . . life is not a spectacle, a sea of griefs is not a proscenium, and a man who wails is not a dancing bear.*

20. Mazen Kerbaj stood on his porch in Beirut & played his trumpet as Israel bombed the city around him—he calls this "a collaboration" & he named this collaboration 'Starry Night.'

19. All acts of subjugation are extreme, while all hierarchies of suffering are false.

21. My daughter has grown up in a country at war, even if it has been mostly invisible to her.

22. *This isn't rock & roll; this is genocide.*

22. Is it extreme to tell your child to step over someone sleeping on the sidewalk? Can the quotidian be extreme?

23. When did it become quotidian to explain to your child that you are angry that a cop shot another black man today & no, you cannot tell her why.

24. At the same time the radio is talking about a boy who jumped off a bridge after being bullied for being gay . . . I tell my daughter he died from being sad.

25. Weeks later she will ask, *Can you really die from being sad?*

26. I lie to her about how her grandmother died; I say she had a bad heart, not that she put a bullet in it.

27. A poem written in a trance can be extreme, depending upon what is pulled up from the subconscious realm.

28. Maybe I have a bad heart.

29. Blake saw the coming apocalypse & wanted to remake the world: *once the Child was fed With Milk; but wherefore now are Children fed with blood.*

30. A mountain can be extreme, if you find yourself trapped on it. A mountain can become a volcano, just as a breeze can become a tornado, and all rain contains a flood.

31. If you string a wire between love & death, you could pluck it & it would be a poem. But if you wrap that same wire around death, it is a bomb.

32. You can of course wrap a wire around love, if that's your thing & it's consensual.

published in *the writer's chronicle*, written as a collaboration with beth bachmann, 2017

nick flynn / maeve flynn, *poison tree*, 2012

THE QUEEN OF THE FAIRIES

This past summer, head to head with my three-year-old
daughter on the grass, staring into the blue, she asked me
where the sky started. It comes out of us when we breathe,
I told her. Then we breathe it back inside us. Now, when
I lie with her in her bedroom, before she falls into sleep,
she opens her eyes wide in the dim light and points to the
ceiling: Do you see that? she asks. That baby bear coming
out of its cave? Amazing, I say, the ceiling shadowy white
above us. Where is the bear going? I ask. She's going to find
her mother, she tells me. O, I say. I'm making that with my
eyes, she says. I have magic eyes.

For the last four summers my wife and child and I have
lived in a 150-year-old barn in upstate New York. I
renovated it four years ago, putting in just enough work so
we could spend the warm months sleeping in it. One night,
when Maeve was one and a half, our second summer in
the barn, an hour or so after she'd finally drifted off into
sleep, the light in her room suddenly switched on (her door
is made up of glass panes covered with a thin fabric)—
then it switched off. Then on. Then off. On. Off. For the
next half hour this continued. I crept to the window—
Maeve was standing in her crib, reaching out to the
switch, then looking around the room as it snapped into
light, aware that she was the one controlling it. She'd
only learned to walk a few months earlier.
        Her room, from a distance, pulsed like a huge firefly.

Maeve wakes up some mornings now, when it's still dark
out, sobbing. *Hot Pepper*, she cries, *come back, please. Hot
Pepper, come back.* Hot Pepper is her little brother, who
lives in Paris, who drives a car with his hands and feet out
the window, who has ears big enough to hear everything
we say, even if we whisper. Maeve is almost four, she has
been talking about—and to—Hot Pepper for almost two
years now. Sometimes Hot Pepper has fifteen brothers,
including Crunch-Crunch and Bailey, sometimes he
lives on the head of an elephant, sometimes Paris is the
lit windows behind our Brooklyn apartment. Hot Pepper
lives there, she tells me, pointing. That's Paris. If she hears
a story about anyone who is bad or mean, she assures us
that Hot Pepper will take care of him—Hot Pepper will fly

in and knock him down, she promises. *I love Hot Pepper*, she says. I pick her up when she misses him, hold her as she cries. *I know, love, I know*, I murmur—*it's hard to miss someone.*

Last night Maeve woke me up, crying. I went to her bed, to comfort her. Where are we? she asked. We're in your room, I told her, everything's all right. Why is the movie so dark? she asked, staring up at the ceiling. Why is it so scary? The room did seem especially dark— maybe there was no moon. I lay my head beside hers, looked at the ceiling with her. What's the movie, I asked, what do you see? A snake is biting my leg, she said, her voice rising again. Make it stop. I looked at the ceiling. Is it just one snake? I asked. Lots of snakes but only one of them is biting me. Make it stop, she repeated. Can you change the movie, I asked, can you tell the snake to stop? Can you make the snakes go back into their holes? Can you make the sun come up? Can you see any flowers? She was quiet for a moment, wide-eyed. It's a little lighter, she said. Any flowers? A few red flowers, she said. Any snakes? Snakes are all asleep now, she said softly. Maybe we can go back to sleep ourselves? I offered.

Why did you give me these eyes? she asked, as she drifted off.

from *The Ticking Is the Bomb*

GRIZZLY BEARS, ELECTRIC BEARS, FIRE BEARS

Grizzly bears, electric bears, fire bears—these three
are the most dangerous bears. My three-year-old
daughter informs me of this. I don't know how she
knows what she knows, yet she knows many things.
Lately it is all about bears. Electric bears? I ask her.
I've never seen an electric bear. If you go into his cave
he will fill you with electricity, she tells me, gleefully.
A fire bear throws fire, he will throw fire all over you
(she is on my lap now, her face right up against mine;
she uses her hand to show me, opening her tiny fist as
it reaches my head, making a fire noise). Fire all over
you now, she says. What about polar bears? I ask. Are
they dangerous? She shakes her head—polar bears,
black bears, panda bears—not dangerous at all, of this
she is certain.

I don't know how she knows what she knows, but
then I don't know how I know what I know either.
Aristotle, in his works, first addressed what we are
(physics), then moved on to how we know what we
are (epistemology). When I found this out I also
found out I've been misunderstanding—misusing
(mystified by?)—the term *metaphysics* my whole
life. The term is attributed to Aristotle (no surprise
there), but not to refer to that which is beyond
(meta) the physical realm, which is how I always
used it, as shorthand for what cannot be measured,
for what is unknown. It turns out that the editor
of Aristotle's works (Andronicus of Rhodes) simply
placed a chapter on the nature of being (ontology,
etc.) after (meta) that first chapter on physics—
ta-da, metaphysics! It was an editorial decision,
which after years of mistranslation spawned whole
branches of philosophy and schools of poetics.

When I sat down to write this morning I had one
phrase written on a scrap of paper—*the hard problem
of consciousness*—which I wanted to get clear on,
before I began my day. I'd stumbled across that
phrase (*the hard problem of consciousness*) while trying
to understand something about memory. This led
me to read up on neurobiology (Ramachandran,

Damasio, Pinker), which led me to metaphysics.
Pinker calls the brain an *information-processing
machine*—an understandable metaphor, but it
feels incomplete. We all agree that the brain is
this profound organism, capable of transcendence
and beauty, but for Pinker this magic all takes
place between synapses—everything is inside
us. Everything. Damasio, in *The Feeling of What
Happens*, offers this:

> . . . in the end, consciousness begins
> as a feeling, a special kind of feeling,
> to be sure, but a feeling nonetheless.
> I still remember why I began thinking
> of consciousness as a feeling and it
> still seems like a sensible reason:
> consciousness *feels* like a feeling, and
> if it feels like a feeling, it may well
> be a feeling . . .

If it feels like a feeling, it may well be a feeling . . . I
left Brooklyn one winter, and took a job which (in
part) required me to read poetry manuscripts for
admission to an artist's residency program (I was
one of several judges). Hundreds of manuscripts, yet
a year later I could remember only one title—*My
Feelings*. It had to be a joke, it couldn't be serious.
I decided, before opening it, that it would either be
utterly naïve, or strangely brilliant. Now I might
suggest a subtitle: *My Feelings*; or *The Hard Problem
of Consciousness*. I wrote it on a scrap of paper before
bed last night, I went to Wikipedia when I opened
my computer this morning. I read about it, then
closed the page, and so this will be from memory:
it has something to do with subjective reality, with
phenomenon of perception, with why a song (*Kind
of Blue*), or a certain color (*cerulean*), or a book
(*Bluets*) affects us as they do. Or, more importantly,
why I (still) watch zombie movies this time of year,
when the days are shortest (*The Walking Dead*).
From the page on the hard problem of consciousness
I linked, naturally, to a page on philosophical
zombies (p-zombies), a new term for me. P-zombies
apparently have all the physical traits of humans,

yet without consciousness. They were invented (or discovered, depending on where you stand) as an argument against the physicalists, who believe it is all inside us, all in the synapses. A p-zombie looks and acts like us, but it is not us—if you poke it with a stick it will say ouch, but it doesn't feel the pain. Thereby, the argument goes, p-zombies prove that consciousness can exist outside of our bodies. Of course there are counter-arguments, as there should be. Just as we might not have had John Donne if we hadn't centuries of mistranslating what Aristotle meant by metaphysics.

nick flynn, *ploughshares*, editor's note, 2012

Ark/Hive
(Sources/Inspirations)

Early on I began looking for people I could work with, someone— anyone—to help me with my projects, though what those projects might be was utterly inchoate to me. Unformed. Uncontainable. Incomprehensible. In college I set a typewriter up in my dorm room— anyone who entered that room had to spend some time on it. You had to make something, leave something. I was trying to know what was essentially unknowable—what it is like to be someone else. What the interior life is like for you. This is an idea I continue to wrestle with.

nick flynn / maeve flynn, *escape*, 2012

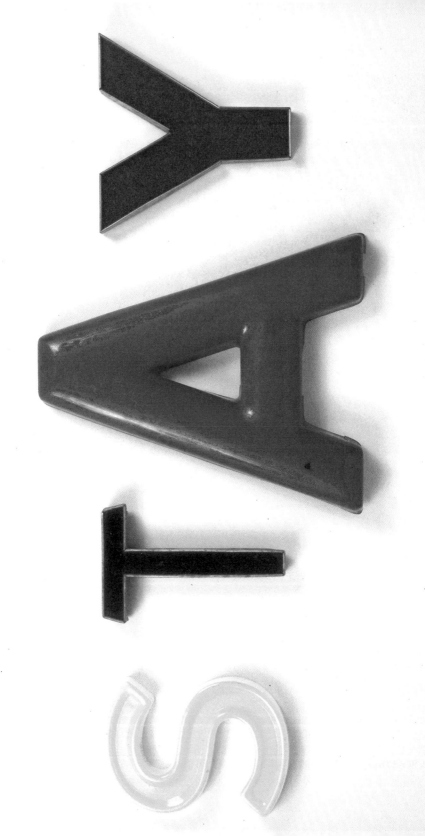

STAY

In the summer of 1991, Jack Pierson lived in
Provincetown, Massachusetts, and spent time
riding around the surrounding water on a
boat sailed by writer Nick Flynn. The boat
was christened Evol *("love" spelled backwards)*
after a 1986 Sonic Youth album, spelled out in
mismatched letters on the stern—the format
that would become Pierson's signature . . .

I happened upon this label next to Jack Pierson's
now-iconic wall sculpture *STAY* at the 2015 New
Museum exhibit *NYC 1993. 1993* was my first
summer living in New York, having moved there
from Boston to go to grad school at NYU. I went to
Jack's show at the Whitney that fall and saw *STAY.*
I was happy for Jack's appropriation of this idea,
which was only partly mine. As Duchamp points out,
"an ordinary object (could be) elevated to the dignity
of a work of art by the mere choice of an artist." Jack
had the vision to make it into something. The idea
to use letters from old signs to spell out the name
of the boat I lived on (a 1939 Chris-Craft—not a
sailboat—and it had no engine, so Jack & I never
sailed around in it) came from my friend Phil Terzis,
whom I'd bought the boat with in 1982. Phil bought
the letters at a junk store & every year we'd give the
boat another name. The name *EVOL* likely came
from my friend Neil Sugarman, who was living
on the boat with me that summer and introduced
me to Jack. Neil would practice his sax on the back
deck. Provincetown was a place that could absorb
anyone, anyone who couldn't fit in anywhere else.
The outcasts, the misfits. Neil went on to form
Daptone Records (home of Sharon Jones, Charles
Bradley, and many others). His Dap-Kings were
Amy Winehouse's back-up band, the sound you hear
on *Back to Black.*

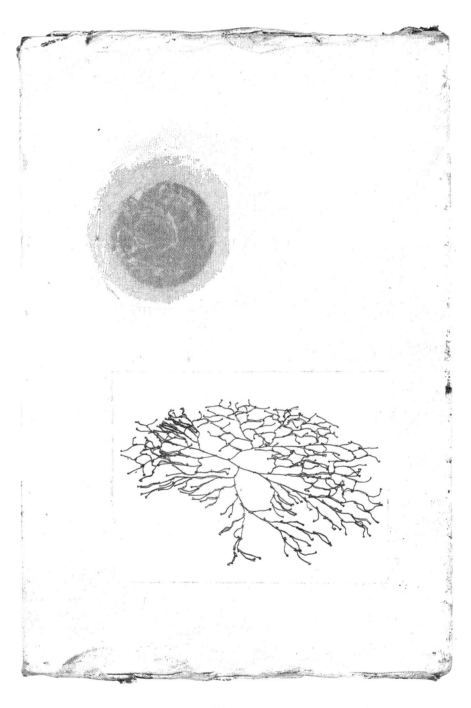

m.p. landis & nick flynn, *mail art*, 1994–2005
(revived 2017)

NICK FLYNN, M.P. LANDIS
& THE U.S. MAIL

Provincetown, August, 1996 M.P. and I cut a
remnant of a ¼-inch plywood in half, making two
panels, each roughly 10 inches square. The plan
is to mail them back and forth to each other,
modifying what the other has done. We come up
with a few rules:

1. We can alter the piece in any way, using
   any materials;
2. We will stamp, address, and mail the pieces
   without outside wrapping;
3. We cannot have both pieces for more than
   24 hours;
4. We will continue the process for one year,
   then begin again.

The plywood is already painted white on one
side. I glue a small paper flag to the center of this side
and mail it off before leaving for Brooklyn. M.P.
draws a series of circles on the un-painted side
with oil pastels. Primarily we want to see if the U.S.
Mail will deliver a piece of wood. It does. We mail
between Brooklyn and Provincetown. The postal
workers in Provincetown seem supportive of the
project; when a piece is brought to the window it is
passed around, commented on. It's unclear how the
postal workers in Brooklyn react, since I mail from
the box on my corner, though early in the second
year one piece never makes it to its destination.

To M.P.'s pastel circles I nail a torn black &
white photograph of an unknown boy, c. 1940. The
other piece is returned with seven holes drilled
through it, looking generally beaten, though the
flag is still intact. Which marks were caused by M.P.,
and which by a hand or machine at the post office,
is impossible to know. The U.S. Postal Service has
become an additional, if unsuspecting, collaborator.

I write across the white of the "flag" piece
with a china marker, something about Horace
Tapscott, whom I'd seen perform that night, and
about a hurricane, which was coming up the coast.
It is not yet fall. M.P. covers the wood with red paper
and what looks like tar, leaving the photo visible,
but threatened. The tar is covered with roses and a
torn seven-of-hearts playing card. Squares of paper
covered with Arabic writing appear over what I'd
written. I add images of a belly button and a car
driving through lightning.

It is important not to be too precious at this
point. M.P. whitewashes over the belly button
and the lightning and scratches the name of our
friend Billy, who had died one year before, into
the white. Each piece becomes a way of measuring
time. I cover the whitewash with oil pastel flowers.
M.P. whitewashes over the flowers. This, I think, is
beautiful, and hold on to it for longer than I should.
I consider saving it, sending him a new piece
of wood. I try to alter it only slightly, taping an
innocuous doodle to its center, but it couldn't last.
M.P. tells me, "You put too much thought into it,

like you're playing chess, like you're making a move."
I send it off, it comes back. The whitewashed flowers
are painted over, buried under garish red house
paint. I begin using sandpaper, trying to get back
to something. The red can't be sanded off.

We are both living in Brooklyn now, moving
deeper into winter. It comes back. I glue fragments
of *Mona Lisa* over blackness. It comes back with *Mona
Lisa* sanded off, three ghost squares marking where
she was, a hole drilled through. I put a diamond stud
in the hole, nail a tin circle to one corner. It comes
back. The tin circle is ripped off, its outline scored
into the paint, the word "TURN" scratched below it.

It's August, the end of year one. Inevitable.
It ends. I like what it's become. I glue a quality
check label to it and put it in the mail. Finished.
Ghostly year. Layered. The places I liked are ruined
now. I like the ruins. M.P. mails me the other piece
for the last time. It is covered with notes we've
written each other—torn addresses, instructions,
doubts, returned now but scrambled, out of order,
mimicking our memory of the year, whitewashed
over and beautiful.

And we begin again.

published in *provincetown arts*, 1999

kevin jerome everson, *blind huber* (film still), 2005

SWARM

When you see us swarm—rustle of

wingbeat, collapsed air—your mind
tries to make us one, a common

intelligence, a single spirit untethered. You imagine us merely
searching out the next

vessel, anything

that could contain us, as if the hive
were just another jar. You try

to hold the ending, this
unspooling, make it either

zero or many, lack

of flurry. *I was born*,
you begin, & already each word
makes you smaller. Look at this field—

Cosmos. Lungwort. Utter each
& break

into a thousand versions of yourself.

You can't tell your stories fast enough.
The answer is not one, but also

not two.

from *blind huber*

SAUDADE

The leaf dropped from the branch

The seed rolled onto the deck
The seedling pushed into the caulking

The sapling split the plank
The tree lifts her into the fog *—beam,*
stem, keel, oar—

this boat, this broken boat, this beach
littered with broken boats *— We have*
come back

from Jerusalem where we found
not what we sought

from *the captain asks for a show of hands*

mischa richter, *poles*, 2010

mischa richter, *harbor* (film still), 2011

HARBOR

If this bowl is always empty

If it breathes if it's lung

If a horse can rise from the ashes

Saul was a sailor on the boat to Damascus

He did not know what he was

Paul turned to a voice it rose up from the waves

It chained his boat to the darkness

A man finds ash & he makes it a man

A horse finds ash in a horse

It lifts us it holds us it breaks us again

It scatters us into the harbor

from *my feelings*

mischa richter, *ray*, 2015

RAY

Ray Nolin was at times difficult, often
        brilliant, always beautiful.
        All of us, those who own one of his
        paintings, or a sculpture, or a draw-
        ing, or those of us who just passed
        him on Commercial Street, will now
        ask ourselves how it came to be
        that Ray died living on the beach,
        living out of his van. It has a lot
        to do with Ray, with his difficult
        nature, but it has more to do with
        how Provincetown has changed since
        Ray first appeared here, sometime
        in the early 1980s, which is also when
        I first started coming.

Where I came from, my hometown, we had
        a couple eccentric folks, guys who
        would wander the streets during the
        day, yet each had a place to sleep at
        night. Provincetown, when I got
        here, had even more—it was a town
        of eccentrics, of outcasts, of misfits,
        of the lost, the damned. And the thing
        was, here, they (we) all had someplace
        to be, even if we had nowhere to
        go—Provincetown was the place you
        ended up in when you didn't fit in
        anywhere else. Then, one by one, the
        most visible outcasts died off—*Anthony,*
        Popeye, Butch—but town was still thick
        with those of us who could pass, most
        of the time. Like Ray.

When I first met Ray he would paint landscapes
        with a palette knife—oils—mostly
        of the dunes. He'd hike in and set
        up and spend all day under the sun.
        He'd wear a broad-brimmed hat, had a
        short blondish-reddish beard, and yes,
        he looked like Van Gogh. When it got
        too dark he'd simply collapse his easel
        and hide his canvas in the eel grass,
        with plans to return the next day. I was
        living on a boat then, and for a while
        Ray stashed paints and canvases on
        board. I never knew when I'd find him
        set up, in the midst of a painting.

I know a guy who'd hike the dunes, searching
        the tall grass for a painting Ray had
        forgotten, or left unfinished. He knew
        it was risky to bring it home, for if
        Ray found out, and he always found
        out, he'd simply break in and steal it
        back. Everyone knew the story of him
        breaking into Berta Walker's one night,
        dragging all his work into the parking
        lot, and building a bonfire with it.
        You never really owned anything Ray
        made—Ray was always working for
        God, not for you, and this was part of
        both his beauty and his difficulty.

He once recited a piece of Scripture to me—
        And God said, Sing me a new song—as
        he was smashing one of the driftwood
        sculptures he'd given me, one that
        had hung on my wall for a year or so.
        Now that he's gone, all of us, those
        who've had to hide one of his paintings,
        those who stole one at some point,
        can now bring it out. And if we really
        understand what Ray was trying to do,
        all his life, we will burn it.

published in *provincetown arts*, 2016

EMPTYING TOWN
—*for ray nolin*

Each fall this town empties, leaving me
drained, standing on the dock, waving *bye-*
bye, the white handkerchief
stuck in my throat. You know the way Jesus

rips open his shirt
to show us his heart, all flaming & thorny,
the way he points to it. I'm afraid
the way I miss you

will be this obvious. I have

a friend who everyone warns me
is dangerous, he hides
bloody images of Jesus around my house

for me to find when I come home—Jesus
behind the cupboard door, Jesus tucked

into the mirror. He wants to save me
but we disagree from what. My version of hell
is someone ripping open his
shirt & saying,

look what I did for you.

from *some ether*

"ON EMPTYING TOWN"

When was this poem composed? How did it start?
It was begun sometime in the early 1990s, when I was a fellow at the Fine Arts Work Center in Provincetown, Massachusetts. It was the first full winter I spent in that town, which can get pretty desolate, wonderfully desolate, strangely empty, by February.

How many revisions did this poem undergo? How much time elapsed between the first and final drafts?
It's hard for me to say at this point, but I usually go through many revisions, especially with a poem such as this, which is basically a collage of three different failed poems.

Do you believe in inspiration? How much of this poem was "received" and how much was the result of sweat and tears?
I think there is such a thing as inspiration, yet without the work it won't come to much, except in very rare instances, the occasional gift. I try to maintain the initial spark in a poem, and then build a structure around it, if that's what is called for.

How did this poem arrive at its final form? Did you consciously employ any principles of technique?
I use a collage technique, the principles of which had to be found (unlike, say, a given form, like a sonnet).

How long after you finished this poem did it first appear in print?
I don't remember.

How long do you let a poem "sit" before you send it off into the world? Do you have any rules about this or does your practice vary with every poem?
Usually I'd never send anything out for at least a year, just to make sure it had actually found its final form. Found itself.

Could you talk about fact and fiction and how this poem negotiates the two?
It's all based on actual incidents from my life at that time, some of which took place in the "real" world, some of which took place inside of me. I hate to break it apart, but here goes: It begins with an evocation of a scene, then moves into a retelling of a troubled friend (he'd probably thought I was the troubled one) who tried to convert me to Jesus, then ends with a meditation on a central tenet of Christianity, that of sacrifice being equated with love. If my friend hadn't left all those images of Jesus around my house, with him pointing at his heart, which made their way into the deep caves of my subconscious, connecting to other violent images from my life, the poem likely wouldn't have found me.

Is this a narrative poem?
It has narrative flashes.

Do you remember who you were reading when you wrote this poem? Any influences you'd care to disclose?
The title, of course, comes from *The Triggering Town*, Richard Hugo's great book.

*Do you have any particular audience in
mind when you write, an ideal reader?*
I try not to think of any reader until
fairly late in the game, but I would like
my friends who wouldn't necessarily
consider themselves poets, though
every word they utter is poetry, to be
able to enter into my work.

*Did you let anyone see drafts of this
poem before you finished it? Is there an
individual or a group of individuals with
whom you regularly share work?*
I was part of a writing group for
years, which was amazingly helpful.
I don't think anything gets created
by one individual.

*How does this poem differ from other
poems of yours?*
The ending is almost didactic,
which isn't something I'm usually
comfortable with.

What is American about this poem?
American? I don't know, the scene
it evokes might happen anywhere, yet
it did happen in a particular place,
which was America, which was the
threshold into my subconscious, at
that moment.

Was this poem finished or abandoned?
I think it found itself, by the end.

brian brodeur talks with nick flynn,
how a poem happens, 2011

journaleach [jur-na-leech) *v.* the process by which the significance of an event or events is drawn out or emptied by excessive coverage in the print and broadcast media. —BEN GREENMAN

jubilee [joo'-buh-lee] *n.* a period of remission from the system of free market real estate, usu. at intervals of twenty-five years, whereby the price of housing is returned to a fixed rate tied to the minimum wage. —NICK FLYNN

Jurassipotamia [jur-ass'-ip-oh-tay'-mi-uh] *n.* a thirty-three acre plot of land in southern Florida that was designated as open roaming ground for the newly domesticated miniature dinosaurs designed by geneticists Van and Rolf Hornblower. The dinosaurs quickly adapted to solitary, independent life and developed and astonishing

nick flynn, *the future dictionary of america,*
2004

ON EXPERIENCE

*Q: How often do the politics of
governance intersect with the politics
of selfhood?*

A: In my first book of poems I
write about a single working-class
mother and a father who's homeless.
I don't know how the personal
can't be political. But the poems
are not prescriptive. What we're
doing in this realm is allowing
the reader to have an experience.
The poem itself is nothing if it's
not an experience, right?

hafizah geter talks with nick flynn,
phantom, 2013

amy arbus, *mourning becomes electra*,
(lili taylor as christine mannon), 2009

WILDERNESS / BEWILDERMENT
(AMY ARBUS & THE SUBLIME)

Here's something: photographs of actors—some onstage, some offstage—*in character*, yet not, at this moment, in the play. Not acting, not exactly, but not not-acting either. Not themselves, but not *not* themselves. Something in between, like the moment between dream and waking, like the moment before the curtain rises, or the moment just after the curtain has come down.

Or maybe it's their day off.

> *When you are working, everybody is in your studio—the past, your friends, the art world, and above all your own ideas—all are there. But as you continue painting, they start leaving, one by one, and you are left completely alone. Then, if you are lucky, even you leave.*
> —Philip Guston, quoting John Cage

A question arises, as to where the character ends
and the person begins, but this is true for all of us,
isn't it? Or maybe I'm simply talking about (or to)
myself again.

Amy Arbus is an artist whose work is, ostensibly,
photographing other artists (actors), which could
risk becoming akin to a snake swallowing its own
tail. Except Arbus, somehow, pushes into the
unknown, into the mystery, not just of theater, but
of the self.

> *Artists don't wonder, "What is it good for?" They*
> *aren't driven to "create art," or to "help people,"*
> *or to "make money." They are driven to lessen*
> *the burdens of the unbearable disparity between*
> *their conscious and unconscious minds, and so to*
> *achieve peace.*
> —David Mamet, *Three Uses of the Knife*

At the theater one is (hopefully) able to be subsumed
into another world, and at the end, when the curtain
falls and you step out of the darkened theater into
the artificially lit city, it all seems transformed. Yet
it's only, it must be only, you, transformed.

> *It's interesting to cut yourself into pieces once in a*
> *while, and wait to see if the fragments will sprout.*
> —T.S. Eliot, in a letter to Conrad Aiken

Longinus claims that the sublime cannot identify
itself only to what is simply beautiful, but also
to what is so upsetting to cause "bewilderment"
(ΕΚΠΛΗΞΙΣ), "surprise" (ΤΟ ΘΑΥΜΑΣΤΟΝ)
and even "fear" (ΦΟΒΟΣ). I've been thinking
about the concept of bewilderment for a few years
now, coming as we are, as a people, out of a type
of darkness, likely generated by fear, where those
we assumed were in charge merely sent their own
shadows into press conferences, to say absolutely
nothing, and the press, their parrots, somehow felt
it was enough to repeat these nothings (*bewilderment*,
1684, Anglo Saxon: from the verb to *wilder*: to lead
someone into the woods and get them lost).

. . . I said, "I am an artist," which I won't take
back, because it's self-evident that what that
word implies is looking for something all the time
without ever finding it in full.
—Vincent van Gogh, in a letter to Theo

An actor, while acting, pushes herself to that
precipice where she is (almost) ready to fall, where
she is (almost) ready to lose herself utterly, and
somehow must pull herself back from it, night after
night. Arbus's photographs capture a group of
actors on the lip of this precipice, about to step into
it. When does the character take over, when is it
ever put away? How often do any of us glimpse our
essential selves, outside of who we've been playing?
Or, as Lear says, *"Who is it can tell me who I am?"*

There are, indeed, things that cannot be put into
words. They make themselves manifest. They are
what is mystical.
—Wittgenstein, *Tractatus Logico-Philosophicus*

published in *provincetown arts*, 2009

jim peters / kathline carr, *studio with black painting & reclining figure*, 2011

WHOSE DREAM IS THIS?

You've been inside this room, you've felt this before. She will, some part of her, always be turning away from you, some part will always be leaving, will never be yours—maybe no part of her, maybe none of her, ever was. Here, in this room, the tv is never on, the bed is never made, no one ever wears clothes, not here, not together. What is this? Simply another annunciation, the moment before what we call God has sent his Angel down to tell you how your life is now forever changed . . . Hold on to that moment, paint it— the before—because once the Angel touches your shoulder, once She whispers the Word into you, it will be impossible to turn back. Back is the ground we once stood on, back is each bent blade of grass (*the beautiful uncut hair of boys*) pushing into your back from the dirt below . . .

This is what happens—imagine walking down a hotel hallway, each

door numbered, the numbers either going up or going down. Someone has just stepped out of a shower, someone has cracked the window, the tv is off. Sometimes you have to keep doing the same thing over & over, even if you couldn't explain to anyone why. Maybe you say, *I am wired this way*, maybe you say, *This is the way the world works*, maybe you say nothing, maybe all of it is true.

written in response to jim peter's work, published in the catalogue documenting his retrospective, paam, provincetown, 2013

david brody, *module drawing A2
for 8 ecstasies*, 2014

BLOOM

No indulgences required, no inner voice

whispering impatiently, no

rough spots—play with these surfaces

& see whether the "sky"

can go further back, can glow more . . . It makes one

pine for gold because

the gold is coming

from *salvaged process notes for david brody's 8 ecstasies*

mel chin, *volume x no. 5 black angel*, 2012

PUT THE LOAD ON ME

This is how it works—the master does not
bow before the slave, he does not

stand naked before her robes, his hands
are empty yet he does not offer—

not even a cupful of—his emptiness
how could he? How could

the world then keep turning? He made his money
(as they say) the old-fashioned way, meaning

he earned it, meaning slaves, meaning
go fuck yourself.

~

A deer (earlier) stood by the side of the road
deciding whether or not to kill me. I cannot

blame her I cannot blame anyone—many
animals were hurt in the production of this book

just as many trees were hurt & all
the clouds. Open any book

& the cloud above you bursts into
flame, you know this & yet nothing

stops you, the sky stuck to the end of your finger
as you point to it.

~

Remember: it's not that everything has to look like
something else, or even remind you

of something else—everything
is something else. This is the story

we've been telling ourselves
since we could speak. *Possess*

nothing, Francis says. *Do good*
everywhere. No one believes

those wings will lift you.

from *my feelings*

ON HURT & CREATION

12TH STREET: *Can you tell us about hurt and creation, and who the deer on the side of the road is in your life?*

FLYNN: Hurt and creation . . . I think for me, if I had to, or could, name that deer on the side of the road, the thing that wants me dead, it would look and sound an awful lot like me. The Buddhists are all about attempting to spread less damage in the world, to walk mindfully, and I guess some of those lines, the ones that come after the deer, are attempts to look at that as well. The idea that trees are killed to publish poetry is an impossible contradiction, yet we write on.

jacquelyn gallo & casey haymes talk with nick flynn, *12th street journal*, the new school, 2016

MEL CHIN / FUNK & WAG FROM A TO Z
(EDITOR'S NOTE)

The book you have in your hands began as a book, or, more precisely, as a series of books—Funk and Wagnalls's ubiquitous encyclopedia, twenty-five volumes, A–Z, twenty-five books that by their uniformity and tone were meant to convince us that therein the world as we knew it at that moment was contained. Not only what we knew at that moment but all we had ever known or done, all the world had ever known or had done to it, and the men (mostly men) who had done it, and all the animals and plants that tried to escape those men and failed. Every home had to have a set, for the children—you were encouraged to pay in monthly installments. In some ways any encyclopedia is a trophy cabinet, wherein the victors are allowed to both display and define the spoils, akin to a wall hung with taxidermy heads—even the word *taxidermy* was up on that wall, between those pages. It was thrilling to hold each volume, and heavy, and impossible, like painting the Golden Gate Bridge—no one would ever get to the end of it, and even if someone did they would simply have to begin again, with the first page. Each page revealed a new world, now alphabetized. But the world changes, and even our way of looking at the world changes, and these twenty-five volumes, which meant so much (or at least were meant to mean so much, or at least to mean something), were now left in boxes on street corners, dusty in corners of give-away shops, forgotten on eBay.

This book you now hold in your hands also began as twenty-five books, but in order for it to again mean anything each volume had to be rethought, rearranged, taken apart, decontextualized, examined, reimagined. Whatever was inside had become merely quaint, or wrongheaded, or irrelevant. Fifty years ago, there were 200,000 sheep in Oklahoma—now, if you were able to take one sheep and place it beside a mushroom cloud, it might begin, once again, to pulse. And if you were to arrange this sheep and this cloud on a black background, the sheep untethered now, the mushroom cloud now blooming forever, both linked now together in this darkness, the background so black it makes us think of outer space, or of the eternal night that awaits. It is said that one of the benefits of our post-postmodern moment is the idea of the indeterminate image, one that forces the reader to participate in the making of meaning. What was once one unified set of twenty-five volumes was broken down into the parts that made it, the elemental particles, and rearranged. Each volume was distilled down and rearranged into about twenty afore unimaginable images, and at some point, twenty-five poets were asked if they might be moved to write something on what had become of each volume. Each writer, it was imagined, would need to have not only these newly created images, but also the volume those images were from, in order to have their own experience with the language, with the smell the pages emit, or simply with holding the book itself, if that was what they needed. Or they could not open the book at all, they could simply look at the images, or simply at one image. As each writer signed on to the project they were mailed a DVD of images, along with the corresponding volume, and a statement outlining the perimeters (the only perimeter was line length, along with a deadline). For a year or so, as these poems were brought forth, the original twenty-five-volume Funk and Wagnalls encyclopedia from 1951 was brought together, once more, yet each volume was on a desk far from the others. One would now need a map to connect them, to bring them together, in time if not space—if there was no map then one could use this book in your hands, which had yet to be created.

My package appeared on my desk a week or so after I signed on. I was assigned volume 10, France to Germany, which seemed perfect, though I didn't know why. I don't know how many others felt that the particular volume and each particular image were somehow picked out specifically for them, as if there were an algorithm into which one could feed all the poems you had written insofar and out would come the perfect set of corresponding images. But this was how it was for me.

nick flynn, *funk & wag from a to z*,
editor's note, 2014

CONFESSIONAL

Lord, I admit you haven't heard from me
in a while. In me, Lord, there's a little
liar. And a little thief. And a little whore.
Forgive me—while writing this poem I was
lost in a trance . . . the sky wild blue, fruit
trees jeweled with ice . . . if not for what I'd

promised, I wouldn't be here at all. You were
with me when I found that box in the basement—
opening it was like entering a room & having
(at last) someone else breathe for me. No one,
as you know, sets out to lose their mind. This
poem began as a secret—not from you, I didn't

know you then. Now it wears its shame like a
halo. Please, take it, rip it up, put it in your glass.
We can watch it dissolve.

from *I will destroy you*

who died and made you king?

(1974) If, without taking your eyes from the television, you call out for a glass of water and your mother, stirring some onions in a pan, answers, *Who died and made you king?*—it might make you wonder if you were, in fact, a king. Unknown, unrecognized, but still—a king. Or, if you call out for a glass of water and your mother, as she passes on her way out, answers, *Who was your slave yesterday?*—it might mean something else. Or it might mean the same thing, for kings, after all, often have slaves, the two often go together, you know this.

In school you study the Civil Rights movement, but you aren't interested in civil rights. You're interested in the Middle Ages, a time of kings and dungeons, which they don't teach in school. *Medieval*, you like to say the word, it has the word "evil" in it. Today the teacher is talking about Martin Luther King—every year you learn the same four things about Martin Luther King—but you are thinking about Nebuchadnezzar, the king of ancient Babylon. God took away his kingdom in order to punish him for his pride, and then God condemned him to live in the woods like an animal. God, apparently, doesn't like one to have pride. For seven years Nebuchadnezzar lived without society or the ability to think. Hair grew all over his body, his nails became claws.

mark adams, *who died & made you king?*
(an activation of *The Ticking Is the Bomb*), 2017

You look at your own hand, stretch your fingers out. Martin Luther King sat in a Birmingham jail, locked up for supporting the right for a man to order a sandwich whenever and wherever he damn well pleased. Your father is in prison, your mother told you so, the prison is in Missouri, but that's all you've heard. From the big map on the wall, the one you stare at when you're supposed to be listening, you know Missouri is in the middle of nowhere. The teacher says that while in prison Martin Luther King wrote a letter. You were supposed to read the letter for homework. *Can anyone tell us one thing he wrote in his letter?* She looks straight at you as she says this—you blur your eyes and she dissolves.

Back home, belly-down on the floor, you read the funnies while your mother reads the obituaries. You look for *The Wizard of Id*—you like Spook, the troll-like guy, chained up forever in that dungeon. You like how every time Spook appears he tries to escape, and you both want him to make it and want him to be there the next time you visit.

One day your mother passes on a letter your father has sent you from prison. In the envelope, along with the one-page letter, he has included a clipping from the newspaper—*The Wizard of Id*. Spook is chained to a wall, a hooded man holding a whip stands behind him.

If you ask your mother why your father is in prison she might say, *Your father is a reprobate.* Since you don't know what a reprobate is, you might think it's a type of king.

But it's more likely that you'll think it's a type of spook.

Your father, from what you remember, from the one time you remember meeting him, looks like a cross between Andy Williams and the Cowardly Lion. All of your mother's boy-

HOME FOR THE WEEKEND

If you rise, someone falls, if you
fall, someone rises. Children come,
children go.

The days are endless here, but it's just
Florida. Speaking of that, *Gone with
the Wind* was on again last week, did
you see it? *Clark. Vivien.* They play it
once a year on television because they
know I love it.

Tara—it must have seemed it would
always be there. I never realized it
before, but when it burns, that's what
brings them together.

Sometimes it's better to simply wait
it out.

Speaking of that, the light coming
out of the lamp in my bedroom is
almost liquid. And loud, like an ocean.
It needs a different bulb. And one.
maybe two bulbs around my vanity
are also burnt out. The light, it throws
my face off. I try to keep all the bulbs
fresh but it's hard.

They lived on a plantation—back then
they knew how to build a house.
Look at what passes these days—no
more tree-lined driveways, no more
verandahs, no more help. The field
hands have all moved into the mansion.
Who did you ride the elevator up
with? This building, I'm being buried
alive in this building. Look out the
window, all these buildings—more
mirror than window, more reflection
than door—they look like they're on
fire before they're even finished.

Listen—it sounds like the ocean is in
the air conditioner.

Sometimes it's better to simply wait
it out, but you need to be ready, just
in case. I go out, of course I go out,
why else would I get ready? A woman
should always be ready. Lipstick.
Cigarettes. Curlers. You never know
who or when the bell will ring. That's
why the dead bulbs are so hard. My
face, it tilts, putting it on, and I need
to be ready. The world is, after all,
a mirror. See these stretch marks?
These are you. It's a fact—children
ruin a woman's body. You left a map
on my body, but not a map I can use.

*Would you mind if I put my hand in
your pocket?* Vivien Leigh, the things
she had to do. Gable was an animal,
a real animal. You can tell all you
need to know by looking at a man as
he walks away from you—watch him
from behind, see how he walks. If I've
taught you nothing else I hope I've
at least taught you that. That, and
that a woman should always be ready.
Lipstick. Cigarettes. Curlers. You
need a mirror but you should only
look at whatever part of your face you
are working on—the lips, the eyes,
the cheeks. It's best not to look at the
whole thing.

Outside these windows it's Florida.
Where do you think the light
comes from?

written for and published
in the catalogue for marilyn
minter's retrospective *pretty /
dirty*, camh, houston, 2014

marilyn minter, *(coral ridge towers) mom making up,* 1969

BALDESSARI / FLYNN COLLABORATION

checklist (agreed upon 9 sept 2005):

a found image that means absolutely nothing to you.

a visual representation of the history of art.

a visual representation of the history of poetry.

a collage made of three random scraps of ephemera found
on the sidewalk within three blocks of our studios on the same day.

a collage made of three images that tells the entire story of our lives.

a doodle made while we speak on the phone for ten minutes.

a list of everything you spend in one day.

a poem made up of five found or overheard lines.

five possible titles for baldessari / flynn collaboration.

a photograph of each other, from memory.

three things they'll have to pry from our cold dead hands.

a sketch of your hand (version of a self-portrait).

nick flynn / john baldessari,
failed collaboration, 2005

note: In 2005, John Baldessari & I were commissioned by Rocky Point Press to perform a collaboration. The plan was to publish a book or broadside of whatever we came up with. After spending an afternoon with him in his studio in Venice, California, I went back to Brooklyn. A few days later I sent him a folder of ideas for possible projects, text as well as images. I never heard from him again.

josh neufeld, *cartoon physics, part 1*, 2002

disasters, arenas

where they can be heroes. You can run back into a burning house, sinking ships have lifeboats, the trucks will come with their ladders, if you jump

you will be saved. A child

places her hand on the roof of a schoolbus, & drives across a city of sand. She knows

the exact spot it will skid, at which point the bridge will give, who will swim to safety & who will be pulled under by sharks. She will learn

that if a man runs off the edge of a cliff he will not fall

until he notices his mistake.

nick flynn, *the wrestler*, 2010

Notes on Racism (Mine)

ON CAUSE & EFFECT

I come to nonfiction because there actually *are* things that happen in the world worth measuring and documenting and honoring. And that are mysterious. There's a physics to the natural world; there's a physics to cause and effect. A person does one thing that causes other things to happen. And if you take control of that and decide, *Well, I'm going to make the thing that happened come before the thing that caused these other things to happen*, it actually changes reality in a way. You're taking on the role of God, and I'm not comfortable with that. What I'm interested in, in nonfiction, is the internal landscape, my internal crazy bouncing against what actually happens in the world, the physics of the world. That, to me, is an interesting tension. There's a world that exists—I know some people believe that the world only exists because we observe it, but that doesn't ring true for me—there's a world that exists, and then there's the way we perceive that world. That may or may not be true—I don't know. I do know that I'm not really steering the ship of this world—I'm steering my perception of it. I'm interested in that, in that tension . . . Every project has a moment when it's completely out of your control and you don't think you can finish it, and I find that thrilling.

patricia weaver francisco &
christopher vondracek talk with nick flynn,
hamline university, 2016

nick flynn, *tv jesus*, 2013

NOTES ON RACISM (MINE)

(2010) We've been green-lit to begin filming *Another Bullshit Night in Suck City*, but someone at Focus is having trouble with the way my father's racism is portrayed in the script. It seems that, along with his sexism & homophobia, my father comes off as a deeply unlikeable character. *Try spending a couple hours with him*, I think. I send these notes to Paul Weitz & Robert De Niro, to help them understand something of where both my father and I come from.

personal note: My grandmother remembers that, as a child, Native Americans—Indians—would come to her back door, dressed in rags, begging for food.

personal note: By the time I was born there were no Indians in my hometown, either homeless or otherwise—the only Indian I ever saw was that guy on tv in the canoe with the tear in his eye.

historical note: In my hometown there is a Cape Verdean community, they live on one street, the same street the dump is on, and when the dump got full, when it came time to find a new dump, the town voted to move it across the street.

personal note: When Springsteen's *Darkness on the Edge of Town* came out my friends joked that he was talking about this neighborhood. One friend's father called Martin Luther King *Martin Luther Nigger.*

personal note: My grandmother would flirt with Manny, who ran the dump, so that he would allow her to pick through the discarded furniture. To us, not to his face, she called him a *boogie.*

personal note: My grandmother always had a bowl of mixed nuts on her kitchen table from Thanksgiving to Christmas—she called the Brazil nuts *nigger toes* . . .

personal note: My mother did not allow us to use the word *nigger*, not ever. Our grandmother would whisper the word *boogie* to us, even when our mother was not around.

historical note: In a soundproof studio Al Green sang, *I'm so tired of being alone*, his eyes turned upward, because up was his idea of heaven.

personal note: My mother called burning down one's own house to collect the insurance money *Jewish lightning*, though this was what she herself did, to my childhood home, while my brother and I were sleeping upstairs, and she was not Jewish.

a note on alternative energy: The center of the earth is on fire, the center of the earth is a planet spinning inside a planet and one of the planets is on fire.

historical note: If you were white and rode through Roxbury in the 1980s, a black kid might yell out, *Hey, that's my bike*, and all his friends would tumble out onto the street and chase you, try to knock you off. The only thing to do was to ride away very, very fast.

personal note: Roxbury was one of the first neighborhoods I walked through when I moved to Boston. Ivan showed me around one summer day, the summer after my mother died. We were looking to score, and we did. (*trivia:* In the film Ivan will be played by Chris Chalk.)

personal note: He's very articulate, my grandfather would say of Ivan, whenever he asked about him, and he always asked about him. *Very articulate* dot dot dot bracket *for a black man* end bracket.

personal note: One night, after working in the shelter, a couple co-workers and I were drinking a beer by the water in Southie. Some kids came up and nodded toward a Korean guy fishing nearby, told us they were going to stab him with his own knife and toss his body into the bay, asked if we wanted to watch. *He's not bothering anyone*, I said, and offered them a beer. I ended up in the hospital with a broken zygomatic arch (holds up the cheekbone), ten stitches in the back of my head, and a broken front tooth.

side note: When I tell this story, some people ask what happened to the Korean fisherman, and some don't.

side note: In Boston a few years later, I heard of a band called Hey That's My Bike.

historical note: A white man drove into Roxbury one night and shot and killed his pregnant wife as she sat beside him in the passenger seat of their Toyota. He then turned the gun on himself, grazing his stomach fat with a bullet. A recording of his desperate phone call to the police played on the news for days, *A black man just shot me and my wife.* A manhunt followed, which eventually led to an arrest, even though the police, in retrospect, all said it seemed clear the guy had done it himself. The shooter worked on Newbury Street, one of the richest streets in Boston, in a shop that sold furs—Kakas, which in Boston is how we pronounce the word *carcass.* With the insurance money, before he was arrested, while the black suspect was awaiting trial, this man upgraded his car—from a Corolla to an Acura.

personal note: This shooting happened when my father was in the middle of his homeless odyssey. Newbury Street is one of the streets my father spent many nights on, in doorways or ATMs or beneath church overhangs, sometimes camping out in the doorway of a fur shop that to this day, whenever I walk past, the word *carcass* comes into my mind.

from *the reenactments*

john mattson (my stepfather) with
peace sign medallion, vietnam, 1969

note: In the summer of 1999, the
filmmaker Beth B flew me and
"Travis," my stepfather (his real
name is John Mattson, a Marine
combat veteran of the U.S. war)
to Vietnam. We were interviewed
in-country on the question of
whether war trauma is passed from
generation to generation (*spoiler
alert:* the answer is *yes*).

THE FRUIT OF MY DEEDS

Thich Nhat Hanh gave a dharma talk about a Vietnam vet, an ex-soldier who came to him, unable to sleep. After seeing a buddy killed, this soldier had put rat poison in some sandwiches and left them outside and watched as some children ate them—and since that day what he did has been slowly tearing him apart. *You have only two choices,* Thich Nhat Hanh told the soldier—*continue destroying yourself, or find a way to help five other children. These are your only choices.*

Thich Nhat Hanh always has a contingent of Vietnam vets at his retreats, at least at the ones he holds in America. As the years pass, more and more are from our subsequent wars. I first met some of these vets nearly twenty years ago, and the time I spent with them convinced me to track down Travis, my stepfather, whom I hadn't heard from in years. Travis had served in Vietnam from 1968 to 1970 as a combat Marine—my mother got together with him soon after he got back stateside. They stayed together for four or five tumultuous years, and then they split up.

The years Travis lived with us I never called him my stepfather. He was more of a wild older brother, just a guy who was around for a few years, who taught me how to bang a nail, how to build an addition without pulling a permit, how to "borrow" a stranger's boat to go fishing—then he was gone. When I found him, all those years later, in upstate Vermont, I wanted to ask him two questions: How did he meet my mother, and how did he find out she had died? I'd brought a video camera to film his answers, telling him, telling myself, that I was making a documentary film—the home movie we never had. Later, I would seek out my mother's other boyfriends, ask them the same two questions. What surprised me about Travis was that he felt responsible for her death in some way. He thought she'd used his gun, which I don't even think is true—my mother had her own gun.

(1999) Four years after Travis and I reconnected, a filmmaker tracked me down (she'd seen my home movie) and asked if Travis and I would be interested in flying to Vietnam to be part of her documentary film—three combat veterans and three of their children, the vets

returning to the scene, their children along to bear witness.
The conceit of her film was to examine if war trauma was
passed on through generations.

Travis turned fifty on a train from Ho Chi Minh
City to Nha Trang.

Three weeks into it we spent a day filming a
single stretch of road outside Da Nang, where Travis
had been stationed. Each night, Travis told us, this dirt
road was destroyed by "the gooks," and during the day
the Americans would hire the locals to rebuild it. Travis
knew, everyone knew, that it was likely that the same ones
who destroyed it then rebuilt it the next day. This went on
for months. It was, for Travis, as if Sisyphus had to hire
someone else to push his rock, thereby denying himself
even that pleasure. The day we were filming, Travis spent
a long time trying to find the spot he'd spent so many days
on thirty years earlier, the exact stretch of road that had
been blown up so many times. He spoke with the other
vets, pointed to the line of mountains in the distance, tried
to line up a photograph of his younger self, standing on
that road, with the line of mountains today. While Travis
was being interviewed I stood under an umbrella, trying to
protect myself from the merciless sun, watching farmers
work the rice paddies on either side of the road. Each
shoot of rice, once it reached a certain height, had to be
transplanted by hand—the bent-over farmers were doing
that this day. Travis needed to stand upon the same piece
of road he'd stood upon so many years earlier. *Maybe we'd
bombed the line of mountain beyond recognition*, José offered—
it happens. Travis finally had to accept that it wasn't exactly
as he remembered. As we drove back to Da Nang we
passed small mounds of rice piled along the edge of the
road, drying in the sun. Some of the rice got caught up in
our tailwind as we passed, rose up in the air, then settled
back down to earth.

That night, over dinner, the director announced
that the next morning we were to visit the site of the My
Lai massacre. It was the first we'd heard of it. The other
two vets were not happy about this and threatened to leave
the film if they were forced to go. *No one will be forced to do
anything*, the director insisted. The other vets said they'd
spent their lives living down My Lai, being called baby-
killers by strangers, and this was not why they'd agreed to
be part of the film. Travis looked at them. *This is what we*

all did, he said. *This is what they meant when they ordered us to clear a village—these guys just got caught.* Travis asked me what I thought. I told him I thought we should go, but that it was up to him.

The next morning the bus pulled up in front of the site of the massacre, which is now a museum, a sacred site. Travis and I walked in together, the camerawoman walking backward in front of us. The other vets and their children remained on the bus. The museum is a small building with framed photographs on the walls, most of the photographs from the *New York Times* or other American newspapers. I remembered seeing a lot of the same photographs when they were first in the *Boston Globe*. At some point Travis told the camerawoman to shut off the camera, that he didn't want to be filmed. Then he walked slowly away from us, talking softly to the translator.

The trip back to Vietnam had been difficult for Travis. He'd only been on an airplane twice in his life—once when he was seventeen and enlisted in the Marines, and again three weeks before this moment. His first days back in-country he couldn't even look a Vietnamese person in the eye, especially anyone in authority, for they all wore the uniforms of the Vietcong. Even the "mama-sans," he couldn't look at them. He told the director a day before we left America that he was planning to bring a small sidearm with him, for "protection." *A gun?* she asked, incredulous. She called me and asked if I thought he was serious. *As far as I know*, I said. She called him back—*Travis, you can't bring a gun with you to Vietnam.*

Fuck it, he said. *I'll buy one over there.*

So Travis and I spent the first few days in Saigon (Ho Chi Minh City) searching the markets for a gun, or even a big knife, but in the end he settled for a bag of marijuana and a massage.

Outside the My Lai museum building is an open field, with small plaques marking the sites of what happened—a spot where some huts stood, a well where a baby was thrown down, the ditch the women and children were herded into. A woman, maybe in her forties, was seated on the grass, her legs folded under her, weeding the lawn very slowly, one stalk at a time. Travis watched her for a while. From a distance I watched Travis watching her.

It was as if she was meditating on each blade, considering whether to uproot it (*And now it seems to me the beautiful uncut hair of graves*). I found out later the translator whispered into Travis's ear that the woman had been a child at the time of the massacre and had survived by hiding beneath the body of her dead mother. Travis nodded, asked if he could speak with her. The translator went to the woman, knelt down, spoke some words, looked back at Travis, gestured for him to come. I watched Travis walk up, say something for the translator to translate. I watched him kneel down before this woman, still seated on the grass, take her hand, kiss it, ask her to forgive him, to forgive America.

from *The Ticking Is the Bomb*

god's loneliness (known)

Soon—very soon—I shall be known: these are the first words my father, locked up for robbing banks, or something like robbing banks, wrote me. His return address was #9567328, Federal Prison, Springfield, Missouri. I often hear myself calling him a bankrobber, perhaps because the word "bankrobber" has more electricity in it than "fuckup." His charge was "interstate transportation of stolen securities"—he'd entered a few banks and said a few words and passed a few bad checks and left with money that wasn't his. In every bank he'd been photographed, smiling into the camera. *Soon—very soon—I shall be known.* Known? What else did anyone need to know?

According to some Sufis, it was God's loneliness and desire to be known that set creation going. When I was still drinking, though maybe not enjoying it as much as I once had (*first the man takes a drink, then the drink takes a drink, then the drink takes the man*), a lover turned to me, her palm flat on my chest—*You know*, she said, *I don't really know you at all*. We'd been together for a few months, likely she was simply expressing a desire to get to know me better, to get invited inside the walls of my invisible fortress, the one I'd been building my whole life.

mark adams, *god's loneliness*,
(an activation of *The Ticking Is the Bomb*), 2017

The thing was, the whole point was that no one was invited in. I might refer to this or that rough patch from my little box of tragedies, hold them up likes slides to a lightbulb—proof— but that was just to get whoever was listening to hold on to me a little tighter. It had nothing to do with them getting inside. Inside this fortress a man was wrestling with his own shadow, muttering that he'd never let himself be surprised, not again. Muttering that he'd never again let himself be tricked into getting so close to someone that he might risk missing her.

God's loneliness and desire to be known set creation going. Unmanifest things, lacking names, remained unmanifest until the violence of God's sense of isolation sent the heavens into a spasm of procreating words that then became matter.

The violence of God's sense of isolation.

Another lover, shortly after I quit drinking, told me that my eyes were dead. Maybe they were, but her saying it pierced that wall again, and at the time I still wasn't ready for it to be disturbed. She was German, and so I forgave her bluntness (*Your ears taste like poison,* she'd murmur as we'd kiss). This was just days before the Berlin Wall came down, and when it did she flew home. A few months later I showed up at her door in Kreutzberg, something we'd talked about since our teary good- bye (*You're coming out of me now,* she'd whispered at the airport, pulling my hand back to her crotch), but by then she was living with someone else.

SYMPOSIUM

I grew up on a saltwater marsh, I'd hike through it every morning on my way to elementary school. I must have allowed myself an hour to get to school, as I stopped many times—to check out the tide pools, to pull up minnow traps, to drag a bit of detritus to higher ground for possible salvage later, in case the tide was high, and my path needed to be even more circuitous.

Now, as an adult, I swim. I prefer to swim outdoors, in the ocean, preferably, in a murky pond if I need to. And so I was perplexed by people in England, or even in New Jersey, who seemed to feel like this disaster (Deepwater Horizon) wasn't connected to them, as if it wasn't the same ocean. I couldn't look at any water without thinking of it. It has always seemed strange that anyone could imagine that this wasn't happening to the entire world, that the beaches of New Jersey were somehow immune, or the beaches of France. Or the oysters of Wellfleet.

The last few days, an hour or so before sunset, my two-year-old daughter goes out into the field and lays in the grass, looks up at the sky. When I see her, I go out and lay beside her, try to see what she is seeing. *It's so beautiful,* she says, her hands reaching up into the blue. She points to every bird that passes overhead, and says, *Look—she's going home now.*

Look—he's going home.

It's been a very dry summer here in upstate New York, not quite a drought, but the farmer down the road is feeding his cows the winter hay, because grass is not growing in the fields, not enough.

Somewhere inside me is this sort of elemental thirst—I can feel it, laying on the dry grass, looking at the beautiful cloudless sky.

Just think of it: we used to kill whales (*whales!*) for oil, just so that we wouldn't feel so lonely when the darkness found us. On my good days I think that, just maybe, a poem can do what a fleet of whaling ships failed to do, or did only temporarily—it can continue to lead us out of our darkness, for years after the ship has gone under. For me, a poem is a living thing, something with a pulse. We cannot force anyone to read our poems, and yet we have to make sure they are alive, so that whoever does find them has an active experience when encountering them. Maybe like my visceral reaction to a whiff of gasoline, both repellent and seductive. Maybe like my daughter, reaching her hands right into the sky.

from "the way we learn to look,"
a symposium on the deepwater horizon
disaster, *gulf coast*, 2010

nick flynn, *maeve, saltwater marsh, scituate*, 2016

ON PLACE

Q: What part does place play in your life?

A: I am, for better or worse, deeply rooted in the northeast of the United States, seemingly by the circumstances of birth, just as my mother and father were, who grew up in the same town as I did—Scituate—and didn't get so very far from it. My father moved up and down the East Coast, but it doesn't seem he strayed too far from the Atlantic, which is also the ocean that defines water for me. Provincetown, for me, was a mythical town, a place which could absorb those who couldn't fit in anywhere else, which is what I often felt. Both my mother and father spent time there, separately, and it is now one of my homes, whatever that means—though maybe it too has become simply a place of memory.

susan landry talks with nick flynn, *run to the roundhouse, nellie*, 2014

FIELD POET

Strange, that we sometimes have to put ourselves
in another place—unfamiliar, foreign—in order to
wake up. Strange in that we wake up every day, just
where we are. We wake up, but before we open our
eyes we say, This is my bed, or, This is my room, or
This is my apartment. This is my corner, This is
my box, This is my cell. My castle, my dungeon, my
iron lung. My armchair, my wheelchair, my coffin . . .
yet we barely remember the moment our eyes closed
last night. Neuroscientists, I've read, understand
sleep, but it's still a mystery why we wake up. Try
this: Lay in bed (box, dungeon, iron lung) with your
eyes closed—can you list everything you would see
on the mantel (sidewalk, floor) if you were to open
your eyes?

Ten years ago now, I made my way to a lake in the
center of Africa, a lake the size of Ireland. I read
that in a guidebook—*It is the second-largest freshwater
lake in the world, it is the size of Ireland.* Since I flew
there from Ireland I thought I would understand.
I went, ostensibly, to help someone I'd just met
make a documentary film, which he described as a
parable about fish and guns and globalization. His
name was Hubert, the lake was Victoria, the fish
was Nile perch. Nile perch is flakey and white and
it feeds soldiers in Afghanistan and lots of folks
in Europe and America and is perfect for filet-o-
fish sandwiches. The guns—well, arms merchants
supply the guns, and the arms merchants come from
the same countries that import the fish. This is the
way the world works. The first night Hubert and I
met, in Rome, he'd shown me some early footage of
what he was working on, and I was so moved that I
offered to meet him in Africa the next time he went.
To help, whatever that meant. But I was a poet, not
a filmmaker—what could I do? I went to Paris—
which is where Hubert is based—a few times in the
months before the trip. To buy equipment, to look
at footage, to be filled in on that part of the world.
Hubert had spent the past ten years in and out of
Africa—to listen to him was like having a veil pulled

back, like waking up. Africa had seemed, from my
reading of headlines, like a nightmare of chaos—
endless war, endless famine, all of it somewhat
incomprehensible. Hubert, with his parable of guns
and fish, was attempting to put things into context.

As a child I hadn't much opportunity to see the
world, we didn't have that kind of money. I had
to learn what I could from books ("When I was
seventeen, I walked into the jungle. And by twenty-
one, I walked out. And by God, I was rich!"), from
Tarzan movies, from *Mutual of Omaha's Wild
Kingdom*. My mother didn't have the money to fly
us anywhere, except once to Montana—Helena—
to stay with cousins for a month. I was eight, and
that trip to Montana is a vivid nail driven into those
days. I learned to ride a bicycle in Montana! We
made Lego fortresses for locusts! On a road trip
to Glacier National Park we stopped at a roadside
stand, bought turquoise and rabbit pelts and rubber
tomahawks from real Indians. In the back was a sad
zoo, with a sad bald eagle bent over in a too-small
cage—that eagle is all I remember. The mountains
were always in the distance, so unlike anything in
our hometown, and we were driving toward them.
Locusts splattered on the windshield, we had to pull
over at every gas station to scrape their bodies off.
By nightfall we would touch a glacier.

Our hometown was Scituate, on the Atlantic
Ocean. We lived on Third Cliff, which was slowly—
sometimes suddenly—eroding into the sea. Each
year a house or two was pulled over the cliff, as the
ocean forced its way inland. I would lay on my belly
on the edge of the cliff, stare into the ocean, try to
imagine eternity. That was when I was awake. Or I'd
wander the saltmarshes, strewn with detritus from
all over the world—parts of ships, brightly colored
lobster buoys, the corpse of a white dog.

Annie Dillard, in her essay 'Total Eclipse,' muses:
*We teach our children one thing only, as we were taught:
to wake up. We teach our children to look alive there, to
join by words and activities the life of human culture*

on the planet's crust. As adults we are almost
all adept at learning it. Yet it is a transition we
make a hundred times a day, as, like so many
will-less dolphins, we plunge and surface, lapse
and emerge. We live half our waking lives and
all of our sleeping lives in some private, useless,
and insensible waters we never mention or recall.
Useless, I say. Valueless, I might add—until
someone hauls their wealth up to the surface and
into the wide-awake city, in a form that people
can use. This is what Hubert was doing on
Lake Victoria, all those years. This is why I
wanted to meet him there, to help. It meant
getting a raft of vaccinations (yellow fever,
typhoid, etc.), it meant taking a pill daily
(larium) that had psychosis as one possible
side effect. It meant not drinking any water
unless it was bottled or had been boiled—it
doesn't help anyone if you get sick. It meant
learning how to work a camera and a boom
mic, to carry the money, to guard the
equipment. It meant, mostly, opening my
eyes. Now Hubert is one of my best friends,
and the footage I saw that first day in Rome
has become the film *Darwin's Nightmare*,
which won twenty-something international
film festivals and was nominated for an
Academy Award for best documentary
feature in 2006. In the credits I am listed as
artistic collaborator and 'field poet,' a term
I borrowed from the Vietnamese, who for
thousands of years included a poet in each
military unit (a field poet), whose job it was
to write poems, in order to give meaning to
each day. In Africa it simply meant I tried to
be fully awake to each moment we were there,
and part of that was to transcribe what I saw.
It was the best I could offer.

commissioned by the poetry foundation,
for the series *poets in the world*, 2012

nick flynn, *chole* (1/7), 2002

THE LAKE IS NOT DEAD

Here's a scene you won't see in the film *Darwin's Nightmare*: Raphael, ex-soldier and ex-fisherman, is now the night watchman at the Fisheries Institute on the outskirts of Mwanza, Tanzania (if you have the film in your hand you are now, or soon will be, familiar with Raphael). Mwanza is a gold-rush town on the southern shore of Lake Victoria, only it is fish, not gold, that brings the young there in search of their fortunes. Usually, though, they end up with only a job, but no one complains. One day Raphael took Hubert (Hubert Sauper, the filmmaker and a friend) aside to ask a "great favor" of him. Hubert, who has spent a lot of time in Africa over the past ten years, expected a request for maybe a hundred dollars or so (the average income in this area is $300 a year, as it is for most of the world), a "loan" to purchase something deemed vital—medicine, school books, a new roof—such requests are common in this part of Africa. Raphael, with an almost comical seriousness, asked only if Hubert could bring him a can of flat black paint. One can of paint—this was all Raphael wanted, yet, perhaps from pride (which is all that keeps one alive at times), it was clearly difficult to ask even such a small favor. Raphael speaks English well, and besides being hired as the translator on the film shoot, he is also an informal teacher in his village. Next to his modest house there is a boulder, which, if a square of black was painted on it, could be used as a blackboard. A year later, when we—Hubert, Sandor Rieder, and I—visited Raphael's village as part of the final weeks of shooting *Darwin's Nightmare*, the boulder now had a black square neatly painted on it, with a few smaller rocks arranged in a semicircle around it. A few English words were written in chalk on this improvised blackboard, this open-air schoolhouse, which took one can of flat black paint to bring into being.

Before we go any further I need to pause for a moment in order to repeat a mantra I've only recently learned:

The lake is not dead.
The lake is not dead.
The lake is not dead.

If you've already seen the film, you'll understand why this is important. If you haven't, then soon you'll understand.

Okay, let's continue.

The question has been asked as to what exactly is *Darwin's Nightmare*. Or, to put it another way, If Darwin were alive today and if he were to have a nightmare, would it look like this film? Would the fish that triggered this gold rush, this Nile perch (*sangara* in Swahili, or *mkombosi*, which translates, ironically, as "the savior"), be part of his nightmare? Would the fact that this fish now devours its own young, having eaten virtually all the other fish in the lake—would this trouble Darwin enough to have nightmares? Would the local people figure

into his nightmare, those who, say, will cut down a hundred-year-old mango tree, which could feed a hundred children, in order to make the fires which will boil a few cups of tea? Are we, the consumers of the Western world (of which the Nile perch is an eerie metaphor), whose bottomless appetites set everything we see in the film in motion, are we the nightmare? One of the great strengths of this film, it could be argued, is that it leaves this and many other questions unanswered. Or leaves them for us to answer, as best we can.

An aside—I spend a lot of my time these days in New York City. From where I sit at the world looks quite beautiful—trees, rivers, crowded cafés. I can buy almost anything I want, if I choose to, if I have the money—everything in the world comes to the markets and shops of New York. It seemed the same in Mwanza, when I first landed. Not that everything could be purchased there, but there was a level of economic activity that seemed heartening, after the languor of unemployment that hangs heavy in other parts of Africa. In Mwanza I saw poverty, yes (I see lots of it in New York as well), but I also saw people working, selling, sitting in cafés playing cards, reading newspapers. Fishmongers and taxi drivers. Cloth merchants and tea sellers. Hubert's film shows all of this activity, all these corners of Mwanza, though many leave the film feeling that nothing positive is being presented about Africa. But the film is full of positive images—Jonathan, the artist, who has lifted himself from a childhood of homelessness and now supports himself mostly by selling his paintings, is a success story. Besides being an artist, he has an apartment, at least for today, and he's not starving. Or Raphael, who has a job, is literate, and more than anything wants his children to have an education. And the lake, the largest freshwater lake in the world, a body of water the size of Ireland— the lake is not dead.

But the film does present a stark picture—at moments the images surpassing anything Bosch dreamed up as he tried to imagine hell. I read the *New York Times*, I read about Africa, about endless hunger and war forever, and shake my head as I fold the paper and turn to my meal. If I'm lucky it's a nice piece of fish. But now I'm part of this film, I was there, and shaking my head has begun to feel a little false, like a pose, like a willed incomprehension. I now know that massive amounts of fish are flown out of Tanzania hour by hour, a country perpetually on the brink of starvation, and now I know that the same planes that fly the fish out fly AK-47s and landmines back in. Endless starvation, war forever. But what am I to do—not eat the fish in front of me? What is an arms merchant to do—not sell weapons? Some days the weight of my willed incomprehension

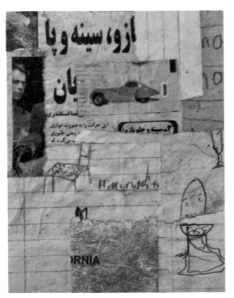

begins to feel like a new form of blindness, a blindness that allows those who are fed to ignore those who are not—an adaptive strategy that might give Darwin another bad dream or two, or at least pause.

Our first days on the final shoot in Mwanza were spent searching for a new crutch for Msafari (his name translates as "wanderer"), one of the homeless boys in the film, who'd lost his leg to a landmine years earlier. Other days were spent in the local clinic, trying to get the doctor to diagnose another boy's chronic cough. In Africa, such tasks are as vital a part of the making of a film as actually shooting interviews. Another part of making a film such as this is the endless conversations, among ourselves and among those in the film and those whose work connects them to the lake. The conversations were an attempt to make sense of what we were seeing and were a part of, trying to hold on to the larger connections that were being revealed—this fish is connected to weapons flying into Africa? Could this be true? And if it wasn't fish it'd be diamonds, set in a band of gold, or the roses we offer to our beloved, all part of a nightmarish cycle that hides within the idea of "globalization."

Les Kaufman, one of a handful of scientists who has studied the biology of Lake Victoria, points out that it is a grave mistake to walk away from this film believing it is too late to save Lake Victoria (and when he says "Lake Victoria" he includes all those who live on its shores), for this will only allow certain corporate interests, with the blessing of certain well-fed government officials, to move in and strip the remaining resources, leaving complete devastation. Les teaches at Boston University, and "The Lake Is Not Dead" is his mantra. As a child I can remember seeing pictures of the American

Great Lakes, the surface thick with dead fish, the
water so choked with pollution that it frequently
burst into flame. It seemed biblical—walking on
water, burning bushes, etc. But we, as a country
(Les and I are both from the United States), put
regulations in place, and now we can again swim
in each of the Great Lakes, and our children can
swim in them as well. The damage we caused was
reversible—is reversible—if we choose to reverse it.
One trouble, though, is that we generate even more
pollution now—certain corporations, predictably,
merely ship it to the Third World, or (even easier)
simply generate it in the Third World, and then
we act as if we can ignore the consequences. Lisel
Mueller has a poem with the line ". . . and one
day Nature declared an eye for an eye and started
pumping our poison back into us." These days,
ironically, this poison sometimes comes in the shape
of a fish.

Thirty years ago, the water in Lake Victoria was
relatively clear—maybe you couldn't lean over
and drink it, but you could see down thirty feet
or more in many places. A tropical paradise, thick
with cichlids—those tiny, brightly colored fish we
generally see only in aquariums—they kept the
lake alive, feeding on plants and thereby keeping
the oxygen balance in place. Six hundred species of
cichlids once lived in Lake Victoria and nowhere
else on earth. Now hundreds of these species await
in labs like those of Les and his colleagues in Africa
and Holland, awaiting Latin names so they can
be given a place on the tree of life, even though
many of them may now be extinct. Hundreds of
species—the largest and fastest extinction event in
human history—ten thousand times faster than the
death of the dinosaurs. Now there is a real danger of
ecological collapse—but remember: The lake is not
dead. Thirty years ago, the water in Lake Victoria
was relatively clear; thirty years ago, Africa wasn't in
the midst of the largest armed conflict since World
War II. Let's add another mantra—Weapons kill.

Near the end of the film Raphael reads about weapons being smuggled into the war zones in the Congo through Mwanza. Raphael reads the article out loud to his son while the camera rolls. There are schools of documentary filmmaking that insist upon merely presenting what is observed, and other schools that recognize that any interaction has consequences. Hubert is of the latter school— Raphael was directed to that article, published in the main Tanzanian newspaper, by Hubert. But Hubert didn't write the article, didn't smuggle in the arms, didn't arrange to have all the fish leave the country, didn't give the children all the glue they sniff, but he also didn't turn away—on the contrary, he acknowledges that his presence has an impact. By doing this he reminds us that the presence of each of us has an impact. For this we are lucky, blessed even, for this is a hard gift, but still a gift.

nick flynn, liner notes for *darwin's nightmare* dvd, 2005

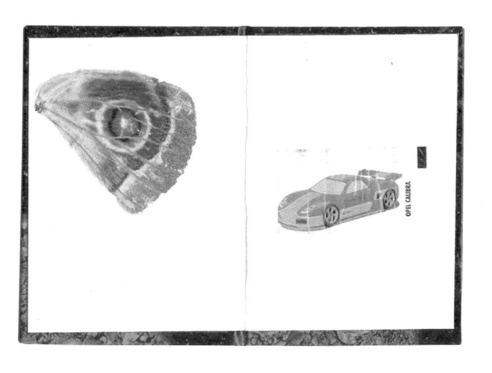

OPEL CALIBRA

CHOLE

In 2002, for a month—maybe five weeks—I found myself on Chole. Chole is an island in the Mafia chain of islands, off the coast of Tanzania, in the Indian Ocean, south of Zanzibar. To get there we flew from the capital, Dar es Salaam (which translates as "house of peace"), a short flight in a small plane, then an even smaller plane to the main island, then a Land Rover across the island to a beach, where we took a wooden sailboat—a *jahazi*—to Chole. The whole trip took a day.

I'd been traveling for a few months at that point, making collages along the way. I didn't expect to find much in the way of ephemera on Chole. The island is remote with no electricity, no cars, no running water, and no roads. The paths, though, were littered with some of the most amazing trash I've ever found, anywhere. Much of it was the same litter, dropped again and again. There were very few products that people could buy on the island. Whatever there was, the wrapper ended up on the ground. Same with pages from school notebooks, even though there was a single, one-room schoolhouse and a notebook seemed like a valuable thing.

What impressed me most were the tattoos that came with each stick of gum: images of cars, mostly, which kids tattooed up and down their arms. (Even though most of them had never seen a car.) What would be the equivalent? Maybe the elephant tattoo my daughter has on her arm.

The kids always tossed the wrapper, which displayed an image of the tattoo waiting inside.

The shop that sold the gum was a vertical wooden box, big enough for someone to stand in. You could also buy cooking oil, rice, matches, candles, bottled water, bananas, and sweet cookies there. I don't know if a sticker of a cellphone came with the tattoo, though I wouldn't doubt it. I imagine the cellphone drawing—a paper phone—came from the image on the sticker, or one like it.

This, after all, is how many things imagined became real, by first owning the image—*own the image and you own half the thing itself,* Jung said. I like the effects of weather, and I also like the effects of someone's hand—a drawing on a scrap of paper, a list written out and discarded, the way paper can have several lives.

I was as far away from my life as I have ever been. If I find more than three scraps I will, sometimes, put them all together and discard one, so that by the end of the day I only have three— that somehow speak to each other, though I don't yet know what they are saying. It's the language of this strange city and island.

first published online in *nowhere,* 2012; reprinted in *nowhere* (first edition print annual), 2017

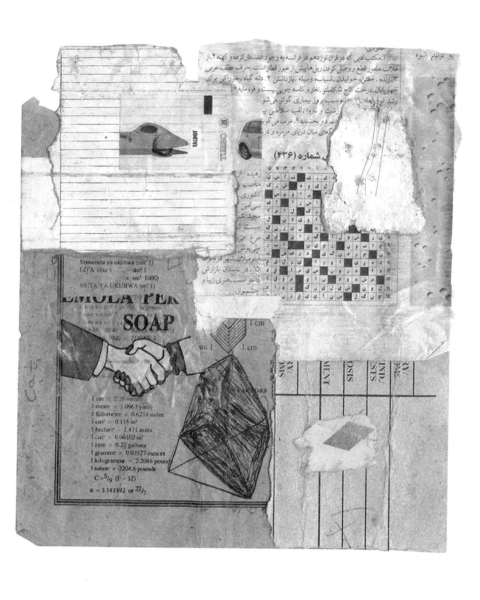

daniel heyman, *I was in the cage 7 days*, 2008

I WAS IN THE CAGE

I woke up, I asked why—
my children, my

wife, my leg. Outside
my head—cold, rainy,

a tent—there were others
I heard,

my brother, a pipe, cold
water at night. They let me

go once, my hands always
laughing

from *the captain asks for a show of hands*

ISTANBUL

(the happy-bus)

It is likely you have seen the photograph of the naked man being dragged by a leash out of a cell by a girl named England—let's call him Amir. This is the third time the lawyers have met with Amir. The first time was in Amman, Jordan, where he told about his years in Abu Ghraib. The second time was six months ago, in Istanbul, when a team of doctors examined him, to corroborate his scars. This time is for him to look through the binders of the now-infamous photographs, to identify who and what he can. A painting on the wall behind his head depicts a scene from Turkey's past—peacocks and lions mingling together in a sultan's garden, a dark-skinned slave tending over it all.

Amir was a businessman awaiting a shipment of air conditioners from Iran when the CIA broke into his hotel room and arrested him. He was in his late twenties then. When we get to the photograph of him being dragged by the leash, he stops. *I remember that night*, he says, *I remember everything.* And then he tells us the story. The lawyer never takes her eyes off his face as he speaks, softly repeating, *And then what happened, and then what*, as he tells of his body being dragged from room to room, cell to cell.

It is only a year since Amir was released from prison. The soldiers called the day of his release "the happy-bus day." *Tomorrow you will get to ride on the happy-bus*, they told him. Today, a year later, Amir shakes his head as he looks at the photographs of himself from that time—*I cannot recognize myself as that man*, he says. *Can you?*

(the word made flesh)

There is a moment in Amir's story, as there will be in every story, when words are not enough, a moment when the only way to tell us what happened is to show us what they did to his body. At this moment he pushes back from the table and stands—*They hang me this way*, he says, and raises his arms out to his side as if crucified in the air. Something about him standing, about his body suddenly rising up, completely unhinges me, something about it makes his words real in a way they hadn't been before. At this moment I get it: these words are about his body, it was his body this

body this story happened to, the body that is right
here beside me, in this room I could barely even imagine
just yesterday, his body that is now filling the air above
our heads, our eyes upturned to see him. Amir stands
there like that, arms outstretched—the scribe has nothing
to write, the painter has nothing to paint, the interpreter
has nothing to interpret, the lawyer's eyes are fixed on
his eyes, all his words have led to this moment, when his
body is finally allowed to speak. The lawyer shakes her
head slightly. *And what happened next?* she says softly, and
he lowers his arms and sits.

(the americans)

At times, in the silence between when a question is asked
and when the translator translates it and when the answer
is given, the only sound is the *clink clink clink* of the artist
cleaning his brush in a glass of water. After four hours
we finish going over the photographs with Amir, and we
are all completely drained. As we stand to thank him, he
reaches into his bag and takes out a camera. It looks so
odd in his hands. He asks the translator to ask us to stand
against one wall—he gestures toward it. We all move,
awkwardly, to one corner of the room, gather together in
front of a painting of a hammam. Amir raises the camera
to his eye and smiles—*You see, it's not only the Americans
who like to take photographs.*

(the man in the photograph)

This is where we pour the words into a jar, as if they were
water. As if a jar of water was the same as a river. This is
where we try to make a coherent narrative out of chaos. As
Amir looks at the photographs of himself, the photographs
of what happened three years ago now, he says, *I do not
believe it was me that was there.* On the table before him is
the wrist tag he was issued, the number he was given, the
letters CI after the number, the code which signifies that
he was picked up by the CIA. He taps the tiny photograph
of himself on the wrist tag—in the photo he has a beard,
and his cheeks are gaunt—*Don't you see,* he says, *this man in
the photograph, and look at me now.* He smiles. I notice that
his arm is trembling slightly by his side.

(a note on racism [mine])

What surprised me the most about meeting the ex-detainees in Istanbul wasn't their descriptions of the torments that had been inflicted on them—after all, I'd seen all the documentaries, read all the transcripts. What surprised me was that before I met them I had somehow created an image in my mind of what an ex-detainee from Abu Ghraib would be like—I pictured someone angry, damaged, maybe tipping toward fundamentalism. And yet each of these men was completely unique, completely human. Each seemed to have taken in what happened in a completely different way, and it still surprises me that this surprised me. What surprises me is that I forgot that each would be fully human, fully complex.

(tawabeet sood)

First the businessman, then the taxi driver, then the cleric (the translator calls him a "preacher"), then the ex-soldier, then the dentist—could they be any more ordinary? We collect their testimonies, the week goes on and on. Now it's a thirty-year-old student, telling of being picked up in a sweep, part of the recent "surge." U.S. soldiers kicked their way into his apartment in the middle of the night, while he slept with his pregnant wife. The soldiers pulled the both of them from bed, shone a light in their faces, asked him a question about a neighbor, a neighbor he didn't know, a question he could not answer. They threatened to take his wife into the next room, alone—*You know what that will mean*, they told him, but still he had no answer. He was then beaten and shackled and hooded and dragged from the house, thrown into a humvee, driven to a landing strip, thrown into a helicopter, until he eventually arrived at a building he now believes is near the airport, either in Mosul or Baghdad. Once inside this building, he found himself in a large room, maybe the size of a gymnasium, filled with black boxes lined up in rows. Maybe a hundred boxes, maybe two hundred, hard for him to say—he was hooded nearly constantly and quickly lost track of night and day. The boxes are about two and a half feet wide, five feet long. He was thrown into one of these boxes, for days, which turned into weeks, unable to straighten his body, barely able to breathe. Every twenty or thirty minutes a soldier kicked the box, or hit it hard with a club, and it made his shackled body jump. Around him he could hear the screams and pleadings of his fellow prisoners— those with stomach pains, those with infections, those slowly going mad. Three years since the release of the photographs, and you can be assured that there will be no photographs of these boxes slipping out. What was once the vaguely directed actions of a bunch of amateurs on the night shift (if, in fact, that is what it was) has become professional, organized, sanctioned. Someone designed this room, someone fabricated these boxes, a memo went out telling the soldiers how often to bang on the side of the boxes, a memo we will likely never see. Among themselves the Iraqis call these boxes *tawabeet sood*, or *nash sood*—black coffins—I can't help thinking of them as the shadows of the flag-draped coffins we were also not allowed—or couldn't—or refused—to see.

(beautiful)

On our last day in Istanbul, during the last interview, I keep spacing out. Bahir was a soldier in Saddam's army, and he does not smile. His story is less seamless, more fragmented than the others, and I find myself wondering if I believe him. It seems he can't remember much. He looks away as he answers, he starts and stops, he stutters. As I will myself to listen, to pay attention, I realize that it's me—it is the last day and I am so full up with stories of torture and this man before me seems like he hasn't made it out all right. He seems damaged, more damaged than the others, and as I listen, as I pull myself back from wherever it is I go, I realize that his story is one of the hardest. *I was hooded for six months,* Bahir says, *they never took off the hood. And I was shackled to the bars for hours every day. And I was naked, the whole time I was naked. I don't remember anyone's face,* he says, *because I didn't see anyone's face.* Listening to him, I notice that I am sweating, I feel like I will faint. His story often just ends, he cannot continue, he needs a cigarette, he needs to stand and walk around, get some air. We take a break with him, we take many breaks with him. During one break I open the binders of photographs, to a picture of a smiley face magic markered onto a detainee's nipple. I walk into the hallway and weep.

When we come back from the break the artist asks the translator to tell Bahir how handsome he is, what a pleasure it is to be able to paint him. Bahir listens as this word, *handsome*, is translated, smiles slightly—his first smile—then murmurs, *Shokran*.

One sometimes needs to be told that one is still beautiful.

from *The Ticking Is the Bomb*; this excerpt first published in *esquire*, 2008

daniel heyman, *I am a farmer*, 2008

I AM A FARMER

A farmer I was, twenty-two
on the ground—hands

feet back fists & blood.
Nine days I was

I walked naked in front

The door closed to breathe
the door opened a crack

The third day would want
the third day she want

My hand stretched to kiss
electric until

I could see my arm &
was still

from *the captain asks for a show of hands*

PROTEUS

Call me Proteus. I live at the bottom of a steep cliff,
down a treacherous path, at the edge of the sea. You can
see me from the top of the cliff, lolling on a flat rock,
staring into the endless nothing of the sea, but to reach
me is difficult. You've been told that I have the answer to
your question, and you are a little desperate to have this
question answered. As you make your way down, you must
be careful not to dislodge any loose gravel, careful not to
cry out when the thorns pierce your feet. You must approach
me as quietly as you can, get right up on me, get your
hands on me, around my neck. You've been told that you
have to hold on while you ask your question, you've been
told that you can't let go. You've been told that as you hold
on I will transform into the shape and form of that which
most terrifies you, in order to get you to release your grip.
But the promise is that if you can hold on, through your fear,
I will return to my real form, and answer your question.

Here's a secret: everyone, if they live long enough, will
lose their way at some point. You will lose your way, you
will wake up one morning and find yourself lost. This
is a hard, simple truth. If it hasn't happened to you yet
consider yourself lucky. When it does, when one day you
look around and nothing is recognizable, when you find
yourself alone in a dark wood having lost the way, you may
find it easier to blame it on someone else—an errant lover,
a missing father, a bad childhood. Or it may be easier to
blame the map you were given—folded too many times,
out of date, tiny print. But, if you are honest, you will
only be able to blame yourself. If you are lucky, you will
remember a story you heard as a child, the trick of leaving
a trail of breadcrumbs through the woods, the idea being
that after whatever it is that is going to happen in those
woods has happened, you can then retrace your steps, find
your way back out.

The question, then, is not how Proteus knows what most
terrifies you, but how it has come to pass that you don't
recognize your own innermost fears. Maybe Proteus is
simply another name for "shadow"—the shadow you drag
behind you with every step, except when you walk
in darkness, when you yourself become the shadow.

One form I take, as you hold on to me with your question, as I refuse to answer your question, as I try to terrify you into loosening your grip, as I try to terrify you by changing into the shape of that which most terrifies you, one of these terrifying forms that I change into is a waterfall.

A waterfall? Who's afraid of a waterfall?

Here, God says, here is your cupful of days. If you don't believe in God, you still get your cupful of days. Some will be spent making love, some will be spent high, some will be spent reading *Ulysses*, and some will be spent alone. Some will be spent around a table, a meal about to be passed, a steaming bowl of rice, some sautéed kale. It's someone's birthday, someone you have known for ten, no twenty years. To your right is a woman you slept with seven years ago—at the time you thought it might work out, but it didn't. Across from you is the woman you are with now, and at this point it could be forever, whatever that means.

Some of the days you are given will be spent in a strange city, and at the end of the day you will know that you have spoken to no one except the girl you got your coffee from, no one except her. There will always be days like this.

Let's just accept that I know your innermost fear, and that I play on that fear, hoping you will let go, hoping you will give up, hoping you will stop asking your question, hoping you will lose hope. This, then, is a vision of me, of Proteus, as both torturer and tortured. I play on your fears, I want you to lose hope, but at the same time you are the one with your hands around my neck, asking your question.

Some Buddhists believe that as you wander the bardo, that realm between living and dying, you will encounter the physical manifestations of that which terrifies you, over and over they will appear before you—this is your karmic debt, and only those who are enlightened will walk unafraid. Some believe that enlightenment often comes at the moment of death, just as it can often come at the moment of birth. Most of us, though, spend our given

time—our handful of hours, our teaspoonful of years—
hovering between these two poles, muddying the water.
Monkey-mind, some call it. *Samsara.*

A friend tells this, perhaps apocryphal, story: while living
in Hawaii, a volcano erupted, and after the initial blast,
which destroyed the top of the mountain and everything
else in the vicinity, the lava continued to ooze slowly out,
over the next several months, so slowly that you could walk
up to the wall of it, put your hand on it, feel its warmth.
How high was it? I imagine twenty feet, more or less. So
high you'd have to tilt your head back to see the sky. The
town my friend was staying in was downhill, spared the
initial blast, but the lava kept coming. Then the scientists
came, to calculate its movement, to predict how long
it would take to reach the village, to mark which house
would be the first to be swallowed beneath the slow-
motion wave. Is this better than a flood, better than a fire?
It gives you time to move out what you most value, time
to move everything, if you are able. If you are able you
could move the entire house, but I had the idea that the
island was small, the village against the sea, the only
option would be to uproot the house and put it on a raft
and float it to the next island. I had the idea that most
simply went each day to the wall of lava, put their hands to
it, hoped it would slow down, hoped it would run out
of juice, hoped it would simply stop.

Here I am—the maniac tied to the chair, before me
is Proteus. I've been told that a bomb is about to go
off, potentially killing hundreds, or even thousands, of
innocent people. As I hold on to Proteus, as I ask him
my question, as I listen for his answer, he transforms—
into a dog on a leash, into a man dancing with panties on
his head, into a bruise, into a madman, into a waterfall,
into a cockroach in a bowl of rice. Into a man strapped
into a chair, into thirty men strapped into thirty chairs,
refusing to eat, thirty tubes forced down their noses.
So here I am, my fingers tight around Proteus's neck,
asking my same question, over and over, as if the answer
exists, inside the maniac, inside the prisoner, inside the
beloved, inside my mother, inside my father, inside me, as
if the answer is there and just needs to be released.

And so here I am, holding my own head, dunking it into a bathtub full of water, repeating a meaningless question over and over, knowing that I will never get the question right.

And here I am, holding my breath, and then letting it go.

from *The Ticking Is the Bomb*

THE WOUND

Afternoon. Evening. Night. Morning.

The Wound is a quiet novel with a war in the middle of it. We begin in a small French village on one semi-eventful day, a day when something that has been lurking below the surface of every other day—a tension from all that has been left unspoken—rises up for a moment in the form of a few wounding words and a thoughtless (sinister? premeditated?) act. Once that dark thread is plucked it leads us back to all we have tried to forget, all we have tried to leave behind. I say "we" because this is a novel that very quickly pulls us into its orbit. The narrator walks us through this incident and its aftermath and then rewinds the frames to when the protagonist (Bernard) was a young man in a war. Bernard came home from that war and this is what he has become—an outcast—he was not able to turn away from what had happened, or perhaps the pressure of turning away has distorted him. The narrator was in that war as well, had crossed paths with Bernard while over there, he carries some photographs of those days, photographs which keep changing meaning the more he looks at them. *The Wound* ends up being about time and the masks we all wear and how blood runs in both directions at once, both away and toward whatever wounds we try to ignore. The tension builds slowly, surely—it takes its time, yet each word, each gesture, is utterly gripping. Within a few pages you know you are in the realm of something magnificent.

Afternoon. Evening. Night. Morning—this is how
Mauvignier divides the book, these are the names he
gives each section—afternoon, evening, night, morning.
It unfolds in one day, until we land in the Night, which
travels, as nights do, through time and space, bringing us
closer to the unknown, the mysterious, the out-of-sight,
the dreamworld.

In *Achilles in Vietnam*, his study of war and its aftermath,
Jonathan Shay proposes that the Greeks wrote their plays,
in part, to try to understand the soldiers coming home
after their endless wars, what soldiers bring back inside
them, what they don't—or can't—talk about. Why Ajax
slaughters all that cattle in that tent, say. *The Wound*
also begins in such a silence, after the incident that is, in
retrospect, both predictable and unfathomable. A small
cruelty that leads back in time to a larger one, the one no
one wants to talk about.

The books that come closest to *The Wound*'s energies
are J.M. Coetzee's *Waiting for the Barbarians* and Albert
Camus's *The Stranger*. Like those masterpieces, *The Wound*
has the feel and texture of inevitability, as if every word
had been floating along the surface of some hidden river
below the earth's crust, all this time. Until this moment
no one had yet found the crack, no one had simply bent
down, reached through it, touched the water. *The Wound* is
contained in a day, and what happens on that day—perhaps
on any day, if we could only touch it—reveals the entirety
of the universe. Something happens, and through it we try
to understand all that has happened.

At the end of *The Wound* you will find a glossary, which
you might like to turn to now. You find words and places
that may or may not help you as you then read the book
(*wadi, harkis, bicot*). Many of the words are from the Arabic,
others are places of battles or massacres (*Verdun, Oradour-
sur-Glane*). Scattered throughout the book are a handful of
images that get returned to over and over—photographs,
masks, stones . . . each one takes on talismanic significance
by the end. In the end it is, perhaps, simply about wrestling
with what it means to tell a story:

Maybe none of that matters, that whole story doesn't matter, maybe you don't know what a real story is if you haven't lifted the ones underneath, the only ones that count, they're like ghosts, our ghosts, that accumulate and are like the stones of a strange house where you lock yourself in all alone, each one of us in his own house, and with what windows, how many windows? And at that moment, I thought we should move as little as possible during our lifetime so as not to generate the past, as we do, every day, the past that creates stones, and the stones, walls. And now we're here watching ourselves grow old, not understanding why Bernard is out there in that shack, with his dogs so old now, and his memory so old, and his hatred so old too that all the words we could say can't do very much.

On the last pages, the narrator is in a car, and it is an echo of someone else trapped in a car in one of the great novels of the twentieth century—the eponymous *Mrs. Bridge*, trapped in her car, watching the snow fall. And here we are in the twenty-first century, holding a book that looks back into the twentieth, to a central event in the history of France, which leads us to Algeria and its war for independence, which sets the stage for our future, "modern" warfare, with street battles, an enemy who looks just like those the occupiers are trying to protect (or subjugate—it depends upon your vantage point), and the introduction of torture as a means to cow a population. The pattern was set in Algeria, and it has been repeated in Vietnam, in El Salvador, Iraq, the Congo, the list goes on and on, with predictably disastrous results. *The Wound* brings us closer into the mind of those for whom the war never really ends, and how they—we—carry these wounds with us into our homes. All of this takes place in the section titled Night, as if it were all a dream, or a long nightmare, one we had yet to escape, because until now we hadn't found the words.

nick flynn, introduction to laurent mauvignier's novel *the wound*, 2014

blue sky committee, *drone alert sutras* (still of
kahn & selesnick), 2014

DRONE ALERT SUTRAS (MEDITATIONS / PROMPTS)

6 AUG 2014

Drone Alert: Two missiles hit a house. "The bodies of the five
people killed were charred beyond recognition" (Pakistan).

Prompt: Read the alert, meditate for seven minutes, then step
outside, lay on your back, and film for one minute the sky above
you . . . just sky.

9 AUG 2014

Drone Alert: Three people were killed and two women were
wounded when a U.S. drone attacked a house in Ma'rib (Yemen).

Prompt: Read the alert, meditate for seven minutes, film for one
minute water, just water.

16 AUG 2014

Drone Alert: Three men were driving along a desert road when a
drone fired missiles at them, killing all three (Yemen).

Prompt: Read the alert, meditate for seven minutes, then get in
car and film for one minute while driving.

1 SEPT 2014

Drone Alert: Ahmed was in the forest. Four drone missiles came out of the sky. Up to eight people killed (Somalia).

Prompt: Read the alert, meditate for seven minutes, then film for one minute something from plant world that is still alive.

11 SEPT 2014

Drone Alert: Four people were killed when a U.S. drone fired missiles at a pickup truck (Yemen).

Prompt: Read the alert, meditate for seven minutes, film for one minute something that's in motion.

24 SEPT 2014

Drone Alert: Ten people killed (Pakistan).

Prompt: Read the alert, meditate for seven minutes, then film for one minute ten approximately identical objects.

gabriel martinez, *AK-47* (film still), 2015

AK-47

a phone rings in a labyrinth

~

this house you grew out of you grew up inside it

~

inside this house a gun was cocked, uncocked,
picked up, put down, aimed, lowered

~

& yes each of us is born with a gun on the wall yes
a gun in the closet, a gun in our hands, a gun to our
heads—you cannot say it has always been this way
but it has been this way for a long yes a long long
time & this way it is now

~

& the path each bullet makes through the air means
only one thing: *I am I am I am I am I am I am*

~

we could melt it down (*could we?*) into nails or bells
or railroad tracks or a tin cup or a steel toe or a
spool of wire or a shovel or a leg brace or a ladder
or a bedpan or scaffolding or a sewing needle or a
typewriter or a hammer or a crutch or brake pads or
a tiny crucifix

from *my feelings*

AFTERWORD: *ALICE INVENTS A LITTLE GAME*
& *ALICE ALWAYS WINS*

One day, a couple years ago, I found myself flying on a
bankrupt airline over a flooded city. I was on my way to
Texas, an itinerant poet off to teach for a few months.
The man next to me was trying to get to the ruined city
we were passing over, hoping to return home, or to what
was left of his home. The airport hadn't reopened yet,
so he was landing in Houston and planning—hoping—
to rent a car, to follow the highway up the coast. After
listening to the story of how he'd escaped the storm, of
what might be waiting for him when he returned, I asked
him what he thought of the federal response. *They'd done
all they could do*, he said—*It was a flood, after all, an
act of God.* I asked if he thought they could have gone in
sooner, stopped some of the mayhem, the desperation.
Leaning into me, he whispered, *If I was black I'd have it
made right now, I could ask for anything and it'd be delivered
right to my door.*

When asked what his plays were about, Harold Pinter once
famously, perhaps facetiously, replied that they were about
"the weasel under the cocktail cabinet." Pinter insists that
he was merely trying "to frustrate this line of inquiry," but
his apocryphal response suggests a certain menace hiding
beneath the seemingly mundane, which could, in fact,
describe at least some of Pinter's work. "For me the remark
meant precisely nothing," Pinter claims, and there's no
reason to doubt him, except for the fact that it could have
been uttered by one of his characters, and thereby perhaps
offers a glimpse into Pinter's subconscious, or at least into
the bad neighborhood of his mind. Or maybe it's merely a
glimpse into the bad neighborhood of my mind, for now it
is me, still holding on to this tossed-off image, attempting
to weigh it down with significance.

If the racism that the man on the plane felt free to utter
were an animal, I find myself imagining, it might look
like a weasel. The storm, it seemed, had pulled back
the curtain on a level of racism that white America
generally prefers to pretend doesn't exist—hiding under
the cocktail cabinet, as it were. After the storm there
followed a brief moment of hope that now that it was

revealed, dragged into the light for all to see, we would, as a nation, rise up and deal with it. But right away some said that what the storm revealed wasn't a weasel at all, that there was nothing under the cocktail cabinet, or at least nothing to concern ourselves with. One local politician even said publicly that nature had in five days done what he'd been trying to accomplish during his entire political life—that is, get the poor people out of New Orleans. In this light, a storm might be viewed as an opportunity. Naomi Klein has recently coined a phrase for this phenomenon: "disaster capitalism." She writes: "Not so long ago, disasters were periods of social leveling, rare moments when atomized communities put divisions aside and pulled together. Today they are moments when we are hurled further apart, when we lurch into a radically segregated future where some of us will fall off the map and others ascend to a parallel privatized state, one equipped with well-paved highways and skyways, safe bridges, boutique charter schools, fast-lane airport terminals, and deluxe subways."

Alice Invents a Little Game & Alice Always Wins is, in part, about the aftermath of a disaster, though exactly what that disaster is remains unclear. The play came about, as nearly everything does, by something seemingly insignificant snagging on to someone's (my) consciousness, or unconsciousness. The insignificant something, this time, was a photograph of the aftermath of a blackout in New York City—lights out, trains dead, businessmen stranded overnight, unable to make it back to Westchester, forced to sleep on sidewalks and park benches. What caught my attention was their suits—very high-end. Not that I wore suits, but sometimes, privately, I imagined that one day I'd be the kind of person who could wear a suit.

Initial speculation was that the blackout might be "terrorist related," but the terrorists were quickly written out of the story, leaving room for other theories. Tapes had recently been released of young Enron workers chatting gleefully about their plan to black out California for a few days, thereby instilling fear which would then justify jacking up the prices. On the tapes two young guns can be heard joking about "Granny having to drain her pension" to pay her bills. It didn't seem so far-fetched that this moneymaking scheme was being replicated in New York, but it seems that the blackout turned out to be merely a symptom of our crumbling infrastructure—a transformer, maybe in Canada, had malfunctioned, shutting off the power to a huge swath of the eastern United States. Simple, old-fashioned negligence and decay, another day at the tail end of the empire.

But those suits—something about the quality of the fabric against the coarseness of a cardboard box lodged itself in my subconscious. I had spent the previous two years shuttling between Rome and Africa—Tanzania, mostly—and I couldn't help but do the math. Some of these suits cost a hundred times the yearly pay of most Africans—I had a friend in Tanzania who had lived for a while on a cracker a day. While I was there the government, in order to comply with World Bank "austerity" rules, was in the process of privatizing basic services. The electric company had recently been sold to a South African firm, and I swore they paid someone to flick the power off and on several times a day, if just to make us appreciate this miracle we were being offered.

I moved to Rome in the fall of 2001 in order to finish a book on homelessness and my father. One morning, a few weeks after I arrived, I woke up with the flu. I staggered outside to get some juice and painkillers to tide me over, and when the door slammed shut behind me I realized I'd locked myself out. A sick feeling washed over me as I remembered that the landlord had told me that there was only one key to that door, and it was now sitting on the kitchen table. I had my cellphone, but it was early, and I knew the landlord slept late. I left a message and got some tea, my head pounding. My Italian was rudimentary at best, and within an hour I ended up in the public park, sleeping on a bench, my battery slowly draining its charge, the landlord still not calling back.

If I hadn't been writing about the years my father had spent homeless, those few hours spent outside might not have hit me so hard. Deep inside I had always been afraid of becoming him, but I hadn't expected it to hinge on something as simple, as obvious, as a key. What passed through my mind as I lay on that bench perhaps passed through a few of those businessmen's minds that night they found themselves outside: What if this never ends, what if I simply never make it back inside? Could it really be this simple, could it be this blameless?

Some say that in dreams all the characters are manifestations of our subconscious selves. Sounds about right to me. Unfortunately (or not), since these selves are subconscious, shadows, we often do not recognize them. Even before Freud, the Greeks recognized this—think of Oedipus and his confusions.

When I was younger I worked with the homeless for many years, gravitating to the "psych guys," as we called them, though for the first year or so when I would write about them in the daily log I misspelled the word *psych* as *psyche*. I could sit and talk to them for hours—much of what they said was impossible, but some of it made sense. I knew even then that I was attempting to access something in my own psyche, some part of my own madness. I couldn't know it then, but I was also waiting for my father to arrive, to step back into my life.

This was the mid-1980s. As more and more people began appearing on the streets of American cities and towns, some argued that we were accepting what would have previously been unacceptable, and that it could be argued that as a consequence of accepting the unacceptable, America, all of us, were becoming psychically homeless. At the time I merely wondered why more of us didn't simply run down the streets screaming, like some of the psych guys I knew did.

The title *Alice Invents a Little Game & Alice Always Wins* is another one of those things that got snagged on my (un)consciousness. It is the title of an experimental film that a friend, the filmmaker Hubert Sauper, told me about but that I have yet to see—*Alice erfindet ein kleines Spiel, das Alice gewinnt* (1989). It was directed by Claudia Messmer, who lives in Vienna. The title rolled around in my head for a while, found some purchase, and kept rising up to the surface.

Something in me liked the idea of this woman, this Alice, inventing a game that only she could win. It seemed both powerful and insane. Alice is also my grandmother's name—Allie—the woman who raised my brother and me, the one who fed us the nights our mother was working late or out on a date. It is likely one of the first names I ever uttered. She was nothing like the Alice in this play, as far as I can tell. In the book I wrote on the homeless I also used the name as a pseudonym for a woman I knew who lived in a box.

Sometimes, when the phrase "Alice Invents a Little Game & Alice Always Wins" was rolling around in my head, before the writing began, I imagined Alice to be a metaphor for America, and her game like a game of musical chairs, with the idea that the music was about to end. Musical chairs always seemed the prototypical capitalist game, creating a sense of desperation and competition among friends. Who is it that gets to take away one chair each time, and where do the chairs go, and who lifts the needle from the vinyl? That was an idea I had in the initial drafts, but in the end the Alice in the play does not seem like the one who lifts the needle from the vinyl, or the one who takes away the chairs. In these pages she is as bewildered as everyone else, if slightly more accepting of that bewilderment, which gives her whatever power she may have. She is, perhaps, simply one of the many who found a way to live without a chair, so to speak, earlier than the rest of us.

Sometimes it seems like this great game of musical chairs we've been playing in America is coming to an end, that the music is stopping more and more frequently, that there are less and less chairs. Not to be apocalyptic, but as I touched on earlier, we did lose a major American city a couple of years ago to a hurricane and then simply left the survivors to fend for themselves. I will admit, though, that it is (perhaps) my temperament to see disasters where others see opportunity—I hear Mardi Gras went well this year. I spent several years working with the homeless, and then several more working in New York City public elementary schools, where half the students lived in shelters. I saw homeless people everywhere, invisible to most—I knew they were homeless because I knew them, or I could recognize the signs.

Alice began as a handful of images, of phrases, which
eventually led to the images and phrases gathering some
energy around them, until they began to generate their
own energy—an image cluster, a closed image system,
which can be a beautiful thing but can also be a dangerous
thing. Think of the idea of torture, which at this moment
in America seems to have a lot of energy swirling around
it, largely as a result of the image of a ticking bomb, about
to explode, and the madman sitting before you, refusing
to reveal the location. This is a very powerful, yet deeply
flawed, image system, and it has led to some horrific abuses.
It is also a flawed rhetorical argument, based as it is on a
hypothetical situation which is unlikely to ever manifest
itself in reality—it is unlikely you will have the madman in
the chair before you, that you will know he has planted a
bomb, and yet you will not know its location.

In the past few years this "ticking bomb scenario" has been
used to justify changing the Constitution and subverting
the Geneva Conventions. It has led, once again, to many of
us being willing to accept the unacceptable.

Sophocles's play *Philoctetes* begins with Odysseus sailing
back to the island he abandoned an injured Philoctetes on
years earlier. Philoctetes, it seems, is the keeper of a bow
which, it is prophesied, is needed to win the Trojan War.
Odysseus sends Neoptolemus ashore to find Philoctetes,
whose gangrenous foot is driving him mad with pain, to
convince him to hand over this bow for the greater good.
The play deals, in part, with rhetoric and the uses and
abuses of argument. *Philoctetes* argues that it is all right to
manipulate the truth for a greater end: that is, to win,
and thereby end, a war. Neoptolemus is not convinced.
In the midst of these rhetorical arguments are moments
of dark humor:

> Philoctetes: (*screams in pain*)
> Neoptolemus: It isn't the pain of your sickness
>   coming upon you, is it?
> Philoctetes: Not at all—on the contrary, I feel like
>   I'm rallying, just now—Oh, gods!

Rallying. These days, the manipulation of the truth feels
smaller, often simply for accumulating more wealth,

which is why it is said we've become too small for tragedy. Now we read books with titles like *Rich Dad, Poor Dad* and watch television shows like *The Apprentice*, which, it could be argued, are simply handbooks to justify the exploitation of others. In *Alice Invents a Little Game & Alice Always Wins* Ivan understands this, Gideon resists it, and Esra is caught between the two. Alice, who may or may not have invented this rigged game, vanishes in the end, seemingly into the television, to become the only one as invisible and pervasive as the air we breathe.

first published in *bomb*, 2007

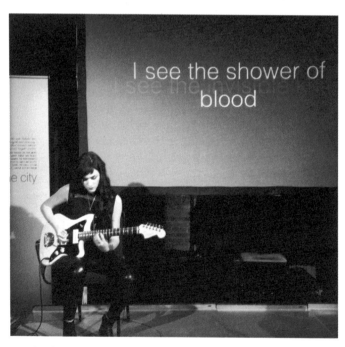

noveller (aka sarah lipstate), *blake & the apocalypse*, manchester, uk, 2017

BLAKE & THE APOCALYPSE

I see the invisible knife / I see the shower of blood
I see the swords & spears of futurity

Sometimes I think thou art a flower expanding
Sometimes I think thou art fruit breaking from its bud

& I am like an atom / A Nothing left in darkness

Tho in the Brain of Man we live, & in his circling Nerves.
Tho this bright world of all our joy is in the Human Brain

O thou art thyself a root growing in hell
Tho thus heavenly beautiful to draw me to destruction

Be near thee loved Terror. Let me still remain
& then do thou / Thy righteous doom upon me.

Only let me hear thy voice

Make me not like the things forgotten as they had not been
Make not the thing that loveth thee a tear wiped away

note: This is an excerpt from *Blake & the Apocalypse*,
a live performance of experimental guitar (Noveller),
film (Gabriel Martinez) & spoken text (Nick Flynn).
Flynn distilled the text from *Vala*, William Blake's
unfinished epic masterpiece—produced by Poet in
the City UK, performed in London & Manchester, 2017.

homeless [hohm'-les] *adj. [archaic]* lacking a home.   –NICK FLYNN

h o r s e c o c k [hors'-kok] 1. *adj.* unnecessarily large, to the point of being vulgar and unseemly. *Steve insisted on driving his horsecock SUV throughout the gas shortage.* 2. *v.* classless over-

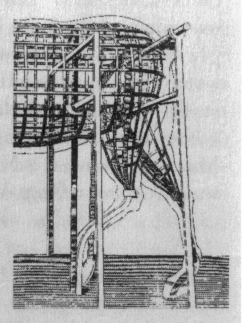

horsecock

nick flynn, *the future dictionary of america*, 2004

The End

nick flynn / maeve flynn,
crow feather flower, 2013

A LIGHT INSIDE (ON PHIL LEVINE)

I think about Phil Levine nearly every day, whenever I sit down to write. He said something to me once—I assume he wouldn't remember, and if he did he wouldn't know the long-lasting effects his words had on me—but these few words set me—my life, my writing—off in another direction than the one in which I was headed. I'd handed in a poem for our one workshop together (at NYU)—I don't recall which poem, or if it ever even became a poem—and after Phil read it he turned to me and said, *You have more light inside you than this.*

By the time I made it to NYU I'd been out of
school for a long time (ten years or so), working at various
jobs (*lousy jobs* as Levine would say about his own jobs in
his twenties, though I suspect neither of us found them
completely, or merely, lousy). I'd been an electrician, an
okay carpenter, a ship's captain (with a bona fide marine
merchant's license), a caseworker with homeless adults. I
liked the jobs, and if I didn't I made it clear and was fired—
every restaurant I ever worked in fired me. My mother
had worked in restaurants my entire life, after working at
her truly lousy bank job all day. She worked nights at bars
or restaurants for the tips, and we lived off her tips—she
drilled it into my brother and me that if we didn't have
enough to tip well, we didn't have enough to go out (which
meant I almost never went out, except to bars, until I was
thirty). During my ill-fated attempts at restaurant work, if
a customer was surly or rude to me I'd go into a silent rage,
or if they tipped poorly I'd chase them into the parking
lot and throw the money at them—clearly sublimated and
misdirected defenses of my mother and what she must have
endured, all those years.

   That I can write about this now is thanks to
Phil Levine—his poems gave all of us permission to write
about the actual, day-in-day-out circumstances of our
lives. That I can actually look someone in the eye and
call myself a poet is thanks to Phil Levine. He made what
seemed an unlikely path seem noble. His definition of
a poet, I once heard him say (on the radio? in an essay?
from a stage? to my face?) was someone who can look
you in the eye—I took this to mean something about
integrity, something about doing the best you could do.
It was not simply a calling, which might suggest a lack
of agency—it was something you had to become, to rise
to, to embody. It would require everything. He once
said (in an interview? in our workshop?) that being a
poet is the one job in the world where you wake up every
morning and nothing you know will help you to approach
the task at hand, which is to write a poem—if you had
remained an electrician, you would know how to get the
lights to come on. But you are now a poet, and each day
you must invent the world. Not the world, but your place
in it. In this Levine is similar to another poet whom I
also think about nearly every day, each time I find myself
in another poem: Stanley Kunitz said that if you read

a poem you like, you must become the person who can write that poem. It is a life's work. How one lives one's life is important. These are things Phil Levine has said to me, over the years, or that he has written in essays, or that I culled out of his poems—it all blurs together now.

In 1992—twenty years ago now—I met Phil Levine in a workshop. It was my second year at NYU—when I first got there I was hungry to sit around a table and listen to real poets talk about poems. I saw it as another apprenticeship, not much different than the one I'd gone through to become an electrician. I was writing like a fiend, in a glorious fever—grateful that I'd escaped the burning house of my twenties (or so I believed). I'd already studied with great poets at NYU (Sharon Olds, Galway Kinnell, William Matthews), but I knew Levine was coming, and he was the reason I was there, though I didn't know it at that point, not fully. You see, I was, and likely still am, a blunt tool, a dull instrument. I need poems drilled into me, I needed to be strapped to a chair. At NYU Sharon had welcomed me into the community of poets and instilled the sense of poetry as a gift (I believe she even quoted Lewis Hyde's *The Gift*). Galway recited Yeats. We'd all go on retreats, the entire class, into the woods, to write. At NYU I got to study with Ginsberg, who cried when he talked about Kerouac, and who hit on me—he hit on everyone who was male. But my last semester Levine was coming, we all knew he was coming (like Grendel), and we knew he would kick some ass. Levine made me want to show up each week and make him pay attention, if only because he didn't let a lazy word or phrase slip past. Anything that was false, or untransformed, or tired, he simply skipped over—he wouldn't waste his, or anyone else's, time. He was exactly what I needed.

I already knew him from his poems, everyone did. *What Work Is* had just come out (I think of it as his *Some Girls*—a masterpiece coming years after his early fury, especially [for me] *They Feed They Lion*). His poems did what I hoped mine would one day do, not only in their seeming effortlessness, but in their unlikely vistas, opening. At some point I read his essay on John Berryman—I identified with him sneaking into Berryman's Iowa workshop, unregistered, with his pride at getting over. I identified with his hunger to learn, after those years of lousy jobs. I identified with the fact that he stuck it out. He found a poet that was his (Keats), just as Kinnell found Yeats, and Olds found Lucille Clifton, and Ginsberg found Blake, and Kunitz found Celan. One line from his Berryman essay stayed with me (this is from memory)—*A poet doesn't play fast and loose with the facts of this world* . . . Levine attributes this to Berryman, but what could it mean? Berryman, after all, had poems with talking sheep in them (*I hope the barker comes*). Look back at the title poem from *They Feed They Lion*:

> Out of burlap sacks, out of bearing butter,
> Out of black beans and wet slate bread . . .

This is Levine both wrestling with the facts of this world (auto plants, race riots), while simultaneously pulsing deeply into its unseen music . . .

> From my five arms and all my hands,
> From all my white sins forgiven, they feed . . .

A poet's job is not to play fast and loose with the facts of this world. What this would come to mean to me is that there is a world, one that demands—requires, rewards— our attention to it, the type of attention Simone Weil describes as a type of prayer. The world is made up of hidden patterns, as yet discovered physical properties, and it is our job to both honor these patterns and to invent new ones. To pulse between seeing and imagining. Berryman's sheep say what sheep would say, as far as we can imagine, if we are able to listen . . .

I cannot claim Phil Levine as my teacher alone— he belongs to many, most notably, and poignantly, Larry Levis, who would die young a few years after I met Phil. Levine's love of Levis was manifest, and generous, and profound. Levine's reputation as a hardass followed him, and was deserved, yet it made his generosity that much more genuine. In workshop, I happened to find myself on his good side, or at least that's how I remember it. If he humiliated me, or my poems, I don't remember. He was committed to the poem, we were being offered the chance to be part of a long tradition, stretching back centuries, we were being invited to gaze into that river with him, to be a part of it.

The poems I was writing then were dark, brooding, gloomy (some might say I still am). Levine turned to me one day, during our weekly workshop, and said that he didn't believe the poem I'd handed in. *You've got more light in you than this,* he told me, looking me straight in the eye. His words pierced me—it was as if someone had really seen me, had acknowledged who I was, had pulled aside my mask of gloom. He did not use the word *luminous*—this is not a word I would associate with Levine—it's not demotic enough, not of this earth. I knew I had light inside me, and that somehow I would have to find a way to let some of it into my poems. It would take me years, but Phil's voice stayed with me, his faith that there was more than darkness inside me, inside any of us. He had seen it (at least he said he did), years before I could.

from *coming close: forty essays on philip levine*, edited by tomás q. morín, university of iowa press, 2012

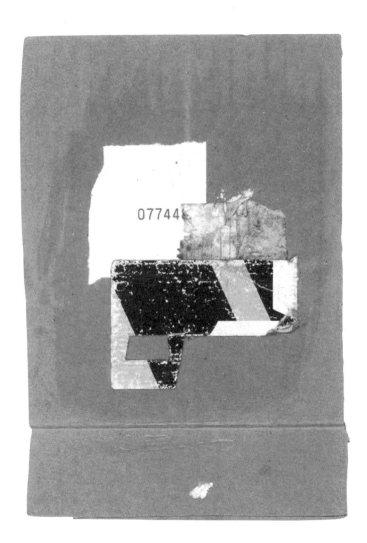

07744

nick flynn, *cage*, 2015

nick flynn, *damage*, 2015

ALL LIVING THINGS HAVE SHOULDERS

For those few years when I worked in New York City
public schools as an itinerant poet—Crown Heights,
Harlem, the South Bronx—I'd lug a satchel heavy with
books on the train every morning. Much of what I
taught was directed toward finding out what the students
saw every day. It was a way to honor their lives, which
isn't generally taught in public schools. The beginning
exercises were very simple: Tell me one thing you saw on
the way into school this morning. Tell me one thing you
saw last night when you got home. Describe something
you see every day, describe something you saw only once
and wondered about from then on. Tell me a dream, tell
me a story someone told you, tell me something you've
never told anyone else before. No one, in school at least,
had ever asked them what their lives were like, no one had
asked them to tell about their days. In this sense it felt like
a radical act. I tried to imagine what might happen if each
of them knew how important their lives were.

In the schools I'd visit, I'd sometimes pick up a
discarded sheet of paper from the hallway floor, something
a student had written in his notebook and then torn out.
Sometimes, I could tell that he'd been given an assignment,
and that he'd tried to fulfill it, and by tearing it out it was
clear that he felt he had somehow failed. Out of all the
ephemera I've bent down to collect from black-and-green
elementary school linoleum floors over the years, one
has stayed with me. Likely it was part of a research paper,
likely for biology. It started with a general statement,
which was, I imagine, meant to be followed by supporting
facts. The sentence, neatly printed on the first line, was
this: *All living things have shoulders*—after this there was
nothing, not even a period, as if even as he was writing it
he realized something was wrong, that he would never be
able to support what he was only beginning to say, that no
facts would ever justify it. *All living things have shoulders*—
the first word is pure energy, the sweeping *"All,* followed
by the heartbeat of *living"*—who wouldn't be filled with
hope having found this beginning? Then the drift begins,
into uncertainty—*things*—a small misstep, not so grave
that it couldn't be righted, but it won't be easy. Now
something has to be said, some conclusion, I can almost
hear the teacher, I can almost see what she has written on

the blackboard—*Go from the general to the specific*—and what could be more general than *All living things*, and what could be more specific than *shoulders?* He reads it over once and knows it can never be reconciled, and so it is banished from his notebook. *All living things have shoulders*—this one line, I have carried it with me since, I have tried to write a poem from it over and over, and failed, over and over. I have now come to believe that it already is a poem.

All living things have shoulders. Period. The end. A poem.

from *The Ticking Is the Bomb*

nick flynn, *panda* (gabrielle greene / alabama song), 2014

ON CAGES

I try to encourage my students to
encounter the world within themselves,
to try to follow the thread they're
writing as deeply as they can into their
subconscious. I suggest that before
they do any research they should spend
time with themselves, however long it
takes: it could be a couple of days or a
couple of years. After that, you might
then be able to encounter someone else
as someone else, apart from you. You
might then be able to allow the world
to enter into you and to become part of
you, to break open whatever cage you've
been rattling around in. But to take it
slow—each moment is interesting: we
have to see our own cages.

robert chodo campbell & koshin paley ellison
talk with nick flynn, *tricycle*, 2013

wayne gilbert, *baby boy brooks*, 2016

THE UNCLAIMED

In every city there's a room

lined with boxes of the unclaimed,
each about the size of half a

loaf of good bread. My friend collects
these boxes, which he then

brings home & opens &
pours into a bucket & mixes with

a medium to make another
painting. One box is

smaller, only as big as a few sticks
of butter, *five days old*

typed out on the label. My friend
does not even open this box, he

cannot, it is heavier than you
might imagine. He simply places it

in the center of a large white canvas
a bit of stardust.

from *I will destroy you*

Many hands have kept me afloat . . .

my six-word memoir from *not quite
what I was planning*, smith magazine /
harpercollins, 2009

THE WORD *WORD*

(usage) It is said that the first book
(c. 400BC) was written in an attempt to
contain every word in the universe—it
is also said that this book is still being
written. *In the beginning was the word,*
which presents the paradox of whether
they are infinite or one, or whether
each book is simply one long sound, or
whether each word fell from the stars
like each atom. We think the word is a
tool to contemplate the universe, but it is
more of an element, dimly understood.
All we are given, all we have, to
understand each word, is other words,
a chain we have been pulling up from
the bottom of a dark lake, all these
years—as each reaches the air we hear
it, but it is part of the word that came
before it, and so meaningless on its own,
much like we are, meaningless on our
own. You can surround yourself with
them, make a cage of them, and only in
this way will you discover silence. And
only silence is perfect.

written for *the lyon lexicon,* a festschrift for
the lyon international literary festival, villa
gillet, lyon, france, 2012

END

Of course it might be a door

or it could be a field or

an ocean

or a glass on a table heavy

with sunlight

& someone there

to hand it to you

a beautiful stone

from the bottom of a river

written to celebrate the tenth
anniversary of the new york zen center
for contemplative care, 2017

kahn & selesnick, *orphelia* (maeve & nick), 2016

impossible without . . . each of the artists who I've been blessed to collaborate with over the years . . . michael zilkha, who came up with the idea for this series & made it manifest . . . ariel yelen, who steadied this project into coherence . . . jiminie ha & with projects, who showed me how to try out some ideas . . . jeff shotts & fiona mccrae (of graywolf) and jill bialosky (of norton), for being such good shepherds of my work over the years & for giving permission to use work previously published by them . . . the editors of the magazines that commissioned work & all the interviewers who wanted to talk about it & the curators who paired me with artists . . . bill clegg, who continues to steer this ship with grace . . . alison granucci (of blue flower arts), who continues to send me out into the world . . . lili taylor, who was & is & will always be an inspiration . . . maeve lulu taylor flynn, who essentially made me who I am & who continues to teach me what it is to be (almost) human . . . *impossible without.*

010 METEOR SHOWERS
. . . like meteor showers all the time, bombardment, constant connections.
—Adrienne Rich, "The Hermit's Scream," 1993.

022 BAG OF MICE
I wrote "Bag of Mice" around 1991, though "wrote" seems too grand to describe the process, as it is one of only a handful of my poems transcribed directly from a dream. It became the first poem in my first book (*Some Ether*, 2000). It would be years before I could even glimpse its deeper psychological significance. My friend Josh Neufeld (son of Martha Rossler, husband of Sari Wilson), who I'd spent a long winter with at the Fine Arts Work Center, transformed this & two other poems from *Some Ether* ("Father Outside" & "Cartoon Physics, part 1," both also included herein) into comics. My only input was that I thought there should be no human figure in any of them, which is how he came upon this shadow.

026 WOOL
First published in *Knitting Pearls: Writers Writing about Knitting*, an anthology, edited by Ann Hood, Norton, 2016.

036 FIELD GUIDE
In 2016, Mark Adams re-imagined *The Ticking Is the Bomb* with his ink drawings over the text. *Proteus, God's Loneliness, Who Died & Made You King?* & *A Field Guide to Getting Lost* are included herein. Mark & I met when I first landed at the Fine Arts Work Center as a fellow in 1991.

041 FIORINAL
In 2004, Paul Weitz acquired the option to adapt *Another Bullshit Night in Suck City* into a film. His first draft was beautiful—weird, smart, moving. My wife (Lili Taylor) read it & said, *This is so good . . . Hollywood will never make it.* It took seven years, three studios & countless rewrites to be green-lit. Paul wrote thirty drafts to satisfy the various studios, each draft, incorporating their notes, a little worse than the last. I read & sent him notes on them all, but in the end, we essentially went back to the original script. The film

ended up with a terrible title (*Being Flynn*, Focus Features, 2012). It stars Robert De Niro, Julianne Moore, Lili Taylor, & Paul Dano. I'm listed as executive producer / artistic consultant, though I wish I'd stuck with my original desire to be listed as, simply, "field poet."

047 AMANUENSIS
First published in *Tupelo Quarterly*, 2017 (italics Robert Desnos).

054 UNKNOWN
Meghan O'Rourke paired Catherine Opie & I up for a collaboration with the intention of publishing it in the pages of the *New York Times Style Magazine*. I offered my poem "Unknown," Opie offered their photograph "For Unknown." Our collaboration appeared as Catherine Opie / Nick Flynn, "A Poet & A Photographer Imagine the Afterlife," 2016.

058 CANOPIC
I read this essay for the first time at the New York State Writers Institute. After the reading Robert Boyers solicited it for—and published it in—*Salmagundi*, 2017.

067 LAST KISS
First published in *Guernica*, a series edited by Brian Turner on "The Kiss," 2016. It was subsequently included in the anthology *The Kiss: Intimacies from Writers*, Norton, 2018.

071 ARE YOU SURE . . .
Are you sure—one would like to ask—that it cannot love you back?
—Maggie Nelson, *Bluets (37)*, 2009.

078 JOE RUSSO
In 1984 I began working at the Pine Street Inn—my mother had died only a year and a half earlier. Pine Street was (and is still) located in Boston's South End. Back then it was described as a "state-of-the-art homeless shelter," yet I still have no idea what that could mean. It seems more accurate to describe it, to describe all shelters, no matter how well designed, as the *perfection of a mistake*. For the seven years I worked at Pine Street my collaborative writing consisted of the daily log at the shelter. I wrote notes for the

oncoming shift, the outgoing shift wrote notes for me. In my off time I took a lot of photographs, made some collages from those photographs, and tried to read as much as I could. *The Odyssey.* Dostoevsky. *Ulysses.* Morrison. *The Woman in the Dunes.* Beckett. *Tell Me a Riddle.* Duras. Baldwin. *Buried Child.* Faulkner. *Enormous Changes at the Last Minute.*

097 ALICE
In 2008 Guy Barash moved from Tel Aviv to New York. Shortly after arriving he found a poem of mine ("Imagination") in *State of the Union,* an anthology of poems written in protest to the Bush (W.) presidency. He tracked me down to ask if he could use it as the text for a piece of music he would write (actually, he had already written the piece). This would be the beginning of what is now a ten-year collaborative friendship. With every book I've written since, some aspect of it has been transformed by the time Guy & I spend together. "Imagination" would become a poem in *The Captain Asks for a Show of Hands,* which is the sister book to *The Ticking Is the Bomb,* both with Abu Ghraib as a central question. *Facts About Water,* a CD including many of our collaborations, appeared in 2014. In 2016 we presented our opera / adaptation, *Alice Invents a Little Game & Alice Always Wins,* at the Fort Worth Opera Festival. In 2017 we began to collaboratively perform poems from *I Will Destroy You.* I'd been performing these poems with my other band, Shaker Flynn (Simi Stone & Philip Marshall) since 2016.

116 TREE
In the late 1980s my friend Zoe Leonard lived briefly on my boat (*EVOL*) in Provincetown Harbor—as I remember it, when she left she told me she was on her way to Alaska . . .

125 MINK DEVILLE
I also read an excerpt of "Mink DeVille Plays the Paradise" in *Heaven Stood Still,* a documentary about Willy DeVille, directed by Larry Locke, 2018.

174–175 THE STONES
Douglas Padgett offered his pencil drawing of *Their Satanic Majesties Request Back Side* as the cover for the issue of *Ploughshares* I edited in 2012. Doug & I met in Provincetown in the early 1980s.

185 MAIL
An essay I wrote on our yearslong collaboration ("Nick Flynn, M.P. Landis & the U.S. Mail") was published in *Provincetown Arts,* 1999. Some of our collaborations were later reproduced in the *Indiana Review* (2005), as well displayed at the Schoolhouse Gallery, Provincetown, MA (2007).

188 SWARM
Swarm is one of a series of short films based on *Blind Huber,* narrated by me, presented as part of Everson's retrospective at the Whitney Museum (2011). I met Kevin in Rome in 2001, where I was finishing *Another Bullshit Night in Suck City,* and he was a fellow at the American Academy.

193 HARBOR
"Saudade" (excerpted herein) is a poem written in collaboration with Mischa Richter's photographs of Provincetown. It was first published in *Provincetown Arts* & was subsequently published as a limited-edition artist's book. For the following three years we performed three other collaborations ("Harbor," "Dragger" & "Ray"). "Saudade" was the beginning of our on going collaborative friendship.

200 JUBILEE
The Future Dictionary of America is a collaboration between a hundred or so writers who were asked to create a new dictionary of hope after the (stolen) election of George (W) Bush (2000), conceived by Dave Eggers, published by McSweeney's Books, 2004.

209 ECSTASY
"Bloom" (excerpted here), is a poem constructed entirely from David Brody's salvaged process notes for his film *8 Ecstasies.* It was published, alongside

Brody's modular drawings, as a limited-edition newspaper, which was distributed at his show *8 Ecstasies*, Pierogi / The Boiler, Brooklyn, 2013. David & I were roommates in Williamsburg through the 1990s—this was our first collaboration.

210 FUNK

"Put the Load on Me" is a poem written for Mel Chin's *The Funk & Wag from A to Z*, an artist book published by Menil Press / Yale University Press. It includes all of Chin's collages from his installation of the same name, as well as original work by twenty-five poets & writers (selected & edited by me), responding to Chin's work. Mel & I met in Houston in 2005, at his retrospective at the Station Museum, and discovered an immediate kinship.

215 CONFESSIONAL

"Confessional" is a cento composed of lines borrowed from Laura Green, Rudean Leinaeng, Susie Deford, Alisson Wood, Jason Lagapa, Emily Stutz, Holly Hausmann, Barbara Sullivan, Camilla Ha, Paula Culver & Phillia Downs—arranged & transformed by me during a workshop at the Omega Institute, 2016.

218 HOME

I met with Marilyn one day in the spring of 2014 in her studio on West Thirty-Sixth Street in Manhattan. We talked for a couple of hours, mostly about the photographs she took of her mother during a weekend in Fort Lauderdale in 1969. As artists, we are connected by our attempts to understand how these people we call "parents" fit into the puzzle that is us. "Home for the Weekend" is a fictionalized reconstruction of our conversation, alongside my own internal imaginings.

242 FIELD POET

In 2001, I met Hubert Sauper through a mutual friend (Rachel Perkoff) in Rome. I was wrestling with *Another Bullshit Night in Suck City*, he was wrestling with *Darwin's Nightmare*. Both projects were attempts to portray difficult realities (homelessness, globalization) in ways that might engage people. Thus began several years of conversations—from Paris to Tanzania to New York. By chance, *Another Bullshit Night in Suck City* was published on the same day that Hubert's film had its premiere at the Venice Film Festival, 2004.

254 CHOLE

In 2002, I flew to Dar Es Salaam to meet my friend Deborah Ash, an international public health doctor, who'd been working for many years in Tanzania. One of her long-term projects, a malaria eradication effort, was based on the island of Chole. I spent two months with her there, assisting in whatever ways I could.

257 CAGE

"I was in the cage 7 days" & "I am a farmer" are excerpts from the poem "seven testimonies (redacted)"—this poem was created by redacting the testimonies of seven Abu Ghraib ex-detainees, as transcribed by the artist Daniel Heyman. Heyman was present for testimonies gathered in Amman & Istanbul from 2006 to 2008. I was present for those testimonies gathered in 2007 in Istanbul. REDACTION, a limited-edition artist's book, based on my collaborations with Heyman, was included in the exhibition *Artists in Wartime*, Swarthmore College, PA, 2010. It subsequently moved to Wesleyan College, Loyola Marymount & elsewhere.

266 SHADOW

Jared Handelsman offered his film *Shadow Landscape* as part of a performance of *Proteus*, Guy Barash's experimental opera with ten-piece orchestration & electronic music, based on *The Ticking Is the Bomb*, presented at Galapagos & The Tank, NYC, 2010.

272 SUTRAS

Drone Alert Sutras is an online collaborative investigation of state-sanctioned violence by the Blue Sky Committee. It was begun by Sarah Sentilles & me in 2014 & is ongoing.

275 AK-47
Gabriel Martinez's film was created in
collaboration with my poem "AK-47"—I
read "AK-47" over the soundtrack.

286 LIGHT INSIDE
My earliest poetry teachers were Carolyn
Forche & Marie Howe—every poem I write
is a testament to their profound influence
on my life. Stanley Kunitz & Alan Dugan
came to me through my time at the Fine
Arts Work Center in Provincetown. At NYU,
besides Levine, I was blessed to work with
Sharon Olds & Galway Kinnell & William
Matthews & Allen Ginsberg. James Tate,
who taught me as an undergraduate
at the University of Massachusetts in
Amherst, exposed me to the possibilities
of contemporary poetry. The first living
poet I knew was Suzanne Gardinier—our
friendship began in junior high, but she
escaped Scituate before I did.

296 ALABAMA SONG
Since 2004 I've taught a studio workshop
class to investigate the idea of
collaboration at the University of Houston,
under the auspices of Karen Farber &
the Cynthia Woods Mitchell Center for
the Arts. My teaching collaborators on
these projects have included Ronnie
Yates, Regina Agu & Gabriel Martinez of
Alabama Song (to see a cool project done
in collaboration with a fourth-grade class
in Houston go to youtube / empty spaces
project: greenscreen, 2006).

299 ASH
I wrote "The Unclaimed" as a collaboration
with my friend Wayne Gilbert, the Houston-
based artist whose medium is, occasionally,
cremains. *Ash,* a documentary film about
Wayne Gilbert and his art, was produced
in 2018.

JACK PIERSON
Evol
1990
photograph

Stay
1991
plastic

JOSH NEUFELD
Bag of Mice
2007
pen & ink on bristol board
w/ computer color

Cartoon Physics, part 1
2001
pen & ink on bristol board

Father Outside
2004
pen & ink on bristol board

MARK ADAMS
Four Drawings:
Proteus, God's Loneliness,
Who Died & Made You King?
& A Field Guide to Getting Lost
2016
walnut ink on book pages
courtesy Schoolhouse Gallery

RACHEL ELIZA GRIFFITHS
black music box with white room
2015
digital print

CATHERINE OPIE
For Unknown
2016
digital print
© Catherine Opie
courtesy of Regen Projects, Los Angeles
& Lehmann Maupin, New York / Hong Kong

NICHOLAS KAHN
& RICHARD SELESNICK
Faerie
2015
digital print

Orphelia
2016
digital print

ZOE LEONARD
Tree + Fence, Out My Back Window
1998
gelatin silver print

ALIX LAMBERT
nick flynn
2007
photograph

BILL SCHUCK
contrails
20015
(detail of installation)

DOUGLAS PADGETT
Their Satanic Majesties Request Back Side
2004
pencil on paper

KEVIN JEROME EVERSON
Blind Huber
2005
film still

MISCHA RICHTER
Poles
2010
photograph

Harbor
2011
film still

Ray
2015
photograph

AMY ARBUS
Mourning Becomes Electra
(Lili Taylor as Christine Mannon)
2009
photograph
© Amy Arbus, courtesy Schoolhouse
Gallery

JIM PETERS / KATHLEEN CARR
*Studio with Black Painting
& Reclining Figure*
2011
oil on wood, lead, cardboard, glass, photo
collection of Nick Flynn

DAVID BRODY
Module Drawing A2 for 8 Ecstasies
2014
graphite on paper
courtesy of the artist & Pierogi

MEL CHIN
Volume X No. 5 Black Angel
2012
excised printed pages from the *Universal
Standard Encyclopedia*, 1953–56, by
Wilfred Funk, Inc., archival water-based
glue, paper

MARILYN MINTER
(Coral Ridge Towers) Mom Making Up
1969
gelatin silver print
collection of Beth Rudin DeWoody

DANIEL HEYMAN
*Iraqi Portrait Series:
I was in the cage 7 days*
2008
gouache on nishinouchi paper

*Iraqi Portrait Series:
I am a farmer*
2008
gouache on nishinouchi paper
courtesy of the artist
& Cade Tompkins Projects

JARED HANDELSMAN
shadow landscape
2015
film still

GABRIEL MARTINEZ
AK-47
2015
film still

IMAGES WITHOUT CAPTIONS
008
Nick Flynn, *Rain*, 1986

012
Jack Pierson, *Evol / Nick*, 1990

089
Mark Adams, *Proteus*, 2016

128 & 139
Alix Lambert, *Nick Flynn*, 2007

174–1795
Douglas Padgett, *Their Satanic Majesties
Request Back Side*, 2004

182
Jack Pierson, *Stay*, 1993

245-255
Nick Flynn, *Chole* (seven images), 2002

264–265
Jared Handelsman, *Shadow Landscape*,
(film still), 2010